102 073 939 8

# A REVOLUTI
# FAMILY POL

## Where we should go
## from here

Clem Henricson

em University
nation Services
from Stock

SHEFFIELD HALLAM UNIVERSITY
WL
306.85
HE
COLLEGIATE LEARNING CENTRE

First published in Great Britain in 2012 by

The Policy Press
University of Bristol
Fourth Floor
Beacon House
Queen's Road
Bristol BS8 1QU
UK
t: +44 (0)117 331 4054
f: +44 (0)117 331 4093
tpp-info@bristol.ac.uk
www.policypress.co.uk

North American office:
The Policy Press
c/o The University of Chicago Press
1427 East 60th Street
Chicago, IL 60637, USA
t: +1 773 702 7700
f: +1 773-702-9756
sales@press.uchicago.edu
www.press.uchicago.edu

© The Policy Press 2012

British Library Cataloguing in Publication Data
A catalogue record for this book is available from the British Library.

Library of Congress Cataloging-in-Publication Data
A catalog record for this book has been requested.

ISBN 978 1 44730 053 3 paperback
ISBN 978 1 44730 052 6 hardcover

The right of Clem Henricson to be identified as author of this work has been asserted by her in accordance with the Copyright, Designs and Patents Act 1988.

All rights reserved: no part of this publication may be reproduced, stored in a retrieval system, or transmitted in any form or by any means, electronic, mechanical, photocopying, recording, or otherwise without the prior permission of The Policy Press.

The statements and opinions contained within this publication are solely those of the author and not of the University of Bristol or The Policy Press. The University of Bristol and The Policy Press disclaim responsibility for any injury to persons or property resulting from any material published in this publication.

The Policy Press works to counter discrimination on grounds of gender, race, disability, age and sexuality.

The Policy Press uses environmentally responsible print partners.
Cover design by Qube Design Associates, Bristol.
Front cover: image kindly supplied by istock.
Printed and bound in Great Britain by Hobbs, Southampton.

FSC
MIX
Board from responsible sources
FSC® C020438

# Contents

| | | |
|---|---|---|
| List of abbreviations | | iv |
| About the author | | v |
| Acknowledgements | | vi |
| one | Introduction | 1 |
| two | The changed landscape | 17 |
| three | What was at the root of it? | 39 |
| four | The legacy and the Coalition government | 61 |
| five | What was wrong? | 77 |
| six | Looking to the future | 105 |
| seven | Conclusion: the proposal and future scenarios | 133 |
| References | | 151 |
| Index | | 167 |

# List of abbreviations

| | |
|---|---|
| ASBO | Anti-Social Behaviour Order |
| BBC | British Broadcasting Corporation |
| DCSF | Department for Children, Schools and Families |
| DfE | Department for Education |
| DfEE | Department for Education and Employment |
| DfES | Department for Education and Skills |
| DH | Department of Health |
| DWP | Department for Work and Pensions |
| EC | European Commission |
| EHRC | Equalities and Human Rights Commission |
| EU | European Union |
| Nacro | National Association for the Care and Resettlement of Offenders |
| NHS | National Health Service |
| OECD | Organisation for Economic Co-operation and Development |
| Ofsted | Office for Standards in Education, Children's Services and Skills |
| ONS | Office for National Statistics |
| TUC | Trades Union Congress |
| UK | United Kingdom |
| UN | United Nations |
| US | United States |
| UK WBG | Women's Budget Group |
| UNCRC | United Nations Committee on the Rights of the Child |

# About the author

Clem Henricson is a social policy analyst who has specialised in investigating the relationship between the state and the family on which she has published widely. She has a particular interest in human rights and has assessed family policy from a social rights perspective in *The contractual culture and family services: A discussion, Government and parenting: Is there a case for a policy review and a parents' code?* and *The child and family policy divide: Tensions, convergence and rights.* She supervised the work of the Commission on Families and the Wellbeing of Children, and wrote its report *Families and the state: Two-way support and responsibilities.*

Clem Henricson was director of research and policy at the National Family and Parenting Institute for 10 years under the New Labour government, undertaking studies for the then Department for Children, Schools and Families, the Treasury, the Home Office and the Department of Health. She led a multidisciplinary academic team of developmental and social psychologists, and cultural and social policy analysts, and developed a model for the future of family services that was instrumental in shaping New Labour's strategic planning in this area.

She now serves on international government and academic advisory committees concerned with family policy, and is a member of the Oxford Centre on Parenting and Children, honorary senior fellow at the University of East Anglia and a fellow of the Royal Society of Arts. She is currently writing a book on morality, tensions in the human psyche and public policy.

# Acknowledgements

During the years of the New Labour government I had the good fortune to work in a national environment that was receptive to new ideas about family policy, and I owe a debt of gratitude to my colleagues at the National Family and Parenting Institute who brought their expertise to bear and worked with me in making a contribution to that debate. There were also many colleagues outside the Institute who were fellow travellers offering much kindness, support and intellectual insight to whom I am indebted. In particular, I should like to thank Andrew Bainham, Alan Deacon, Ilan Katz, Margaret O'Brien, Simon Richey, Sir Michael Rutter, Susan Taylor, David Utting and Sir William Utting. I am also extremely grateful to Andrew Bainham and Alan Deacon for commenting so thoughtfully and helpfully on this book as it came to fruition.

# ONE

# Introduction

Moving into 2011/12, progressive politics finds itself at a strange juncture. Feelings of fin de siècle abound as a cadre of middle-way social improvers move out of influence following the end of the New Labour government and its replacement by a right of centre Coalition. Not only is there a change of elite, but also the slipping from view of a philosophy of government. And all this is happening at a time of economic crisis, lacing the experience with something of a sense of doom.

How should progressives react? First, before there is an irretrievable disappearance from collective memory, opportunities should be taken to review the decade of public policy under New Labour – reflecting on the way it was, in order to inform the way it might be in the future.

What will this period of Labour administration be remembered for? On current form, it looks as though the financial crisis and foreign policy – Iraq, Afghanistan – will hold the headlines. The retrospective narrative as it currently stands, then, is a far cry from the sophisticated and wide-ranging political philosophy that was honed in opposition as a prelude to a decade of power. There was communitarianism, social capital, the reduction of child poverty – and indeed a shift in family policy, which is the subject of this book. And that 'philosophy' was not just hot air. It resulted in some very real achievements.

Well, exits are often accompanied by negative distortion, an uncomfortable aspect of the historical cycle. A further uncomfortable truth is that there are periods of fallow in progressive thinking, and it may be that there will be such a phase now. The direction of the current government does not give ground for optimism as it operates without a coherent philosophy, offering instead an ad hoc amalgam of social welfare contraction and civil libertarianism. Certainly there is no plotted articulated way forward for the future progressive agenda, and perhaps there cannot be until we have a fuller and more balanced retrospective assessment of the recent past.

This is particularly needed for family policy which was one of the principal and most innovative areas of development typifying the New Labour era, and which, if neglected, is in danger of being eclipsed in the long as well as the short term. The philosophy of the interface between public policy and family, and the complexity of its rationale, has all but disappeared from discussion as the current Labour opposition is relegated to parrying accusations over the deficit and treading the tightrope of negative/positive responses to cuts. It has found itself engaging with Big Society rhetoric rather than staking out its own progressive territory.

This policy book is intended to counter the current deficit in thinking on family. It provides an overarching analysis of the philosophy, direction and implementation of family policy since 1997, and draws on this analysis in developing a set of proposals for the next era. It teases out the concept of family policy and sets out a framework for its formulation.

## What is in a concept and why have a family policy at all?

Pragmatists, empiricists and those engaged in the practical delivery of services may shy away from a focus on policy concepts, and certainly there is a risk from over-absorption in the minutiae of conceptual analysis; it can deflect from getting on with the job. Nevertheless there are dangers where too loose a definition undermines transparency and clarity of purpose in government. The importance, for example, of clarity in the separation of powers – legislative, executive and judicial – is widely recognised if government is to function effectively. The problems associated with ill-defined government departmental remits in terms of misconceptions about who is responsible for what and associated buck passing are also all too familiar. There will always be some overlap between different functions of government and, whichever way the administrative cake is cut, there will be some level of dissatisfaction or point of dispute. Nevertheless, the definition endeavour is worthwhile in order to maximise openness and clarity of purpose in government operations.

It is particularly important for family policy which has the potential to encompass most of public policy – or very little. It has been a slippery commodity, and its very fluidity has enabled governments in different countries and at different points in time to use it for a wide range of political ends, from fertility manipulation through to changing class and economic relations. Undefined, there is a risk that governments will entertain grandiose, excessive goals for family policy, and this, as we shall see, took place in the UK. There is also greater potential for domination by particular interest groups or fads. For example, the argument has been made that there has been absorption with child welfare over the past decade to the detriment of a balanced policy approach across the generations, promoting an inclusive family perspective.

The transparency associated with clearly defined policy concepts also has purchase as a value in government. It enables citizens to have an awareness of what they can expect in their dealings with administrators, and an awareness of what they can expect to be done in their name.

Working on the premise that there is benefit to be derived from defining the purpose and parameters of family policy, the first point of reference is to establish what a family is in this context of public administration. Of course a family may be widely or narrowly drawn in the realm of emotions and relationships. Closeness and support may be derived from friendship, but from the state's perspective, because there is no legal or community expectation that support will be delivered via this relationship, friendship cannot constitute a family unit. The point of 'family' for public administration is that it carries with it caring responsibilities and dependency that in some instances can be enforced. The following definition spanning family responsibilities across the generations is put forward with the intent of providing a springboard for developing a family policy in the future that is more clearly defined than it has been in the past:

> The family is a social unit where there is a legal or customary expectation by the state of unremunerated family support and caring, specifically:
>
> - a legally recognised parent–child relationship (whether biological or social) and/or
> - a legally recognised adult couple relationship.

The family as defined here has legally and commonly established functions of caring and interdependency on which the community as a whole is reliant. They range from financial obligations to physical and mental hands-on care. The legal obligations of care directed from a parent, whether biological or social, to a child are underwritten in a variety of legal instruments and addressed in child protection legislation and procedures. Care directed from a child to an adult features less in law, but there are established expectations that children will care for parents in old age, and the operation of elder care is highly significant in its impact on family functioning. Legally recognised adult couple relationships through marriage and civil partnerships also bring with them obligations of mutual financial support and expectations of physical and emotional care. With these functions of caring interdependency, families need regulation and support, and family policy is critical to delivering that regulation and support in a coherent, fair and equitable fashion.

An additional dimension to the need for a family policy is the concentration within this caring and interdependent unit of the most raw and potent of human emotions and behaviours. Families sustain the core human tension of affection, empathy on the one hand, and aggression, deception and self-interest on the other. The tension exists individually between members of a family, but also collectively between the genders and the generations. It permeates family relationships and the management of this tension is one of the principal reasons why we need a family policy.

And yet this rationale is seldom articulated. While the apparatus for addressing divergent interests exists in different pockets of government – criminal justice, family law, child protection, social care and more – the crux of the tension within families is seldom alluded to. Possibly this is because it is an uncomfortable proposition in a society that has a belief system lodged in the enlightenment and the presumption of the perfectibility of man. The aspiration in this mind set is that things are going to get better in contrast to the rather more modest intention of managing an immutable tension. The proposition in this book is that there are benefits to be had from realism, in recognising the tension in family life, engaging with it and developing a policy response – a family policy – that spans inter-gender and generational relationships.

## History of family policy in Europe

The history of family policy since the Second World War has been one of extraordinary fluidity. Its locus across a range of welfare and regulatory government functions has rendered it subject to predominant and shifting public policy concerns. This in turn has influenced a variety and evolving set of internationally applied typologies interpreting divergence and convergence within different countries and shedding considerable light on the socio-political forces at work in formulating family policy.

These analyses have shown the slow development of family policy compared with other social policy streams that contributed to the emergent post-war European welfare states. The emphasis in this early post-war period was on worker-related health and welfare, and something of a legacy can be seen in the circumscribed role of the European Union (EU) in family policy, with its focus on labour mobility still in evidence. The family dimension was eclipsed and, as Esping-Andersen (1999, p 54) commented, these new welfare states fell short in that they 'did not absorb the family caring burden'. The redress of this omission then began to gain momentum as new social risks became apparent as points for concern. These related to post-industrial socio-economic trends with varied employment patterns and work–life reconciliation needs escalating as the male breadwinner model declined in favour of dual household earner relationships (Blum and Rille-Pfeiffer, 2010).

A range of social policies have always had an impact on family wellbeing, so the question for analysis has been how far the family dimension has been considered in policy development. In its analysis of family policy across the EU, FAMILYPLATFORM found growing levels of articulated concern for families. Faced with an ageing population, problems with fertility, social liberation, new family forms, changing work patterns and shifting gender and caring roles, governments have had to develop policy responses (Wall et al, 2010).

Commonly, however, in developing their responses governments have not conceived of family policy in an holistic fashion. Even where family policies have been explicit, they have tended to be motivated by a single issue of principal concern. Kaufmann (2000) has identified the following range of governmental drivers: institutional, demographic, economic, socio-political, gender equality and children's welfare. France, for example, had a strong pre-occupation with fertility rates, adopting a pro-natal stance, while gender equality was a major motivational factor in Scandinavia.

Blum and Rille-Pfeiffer (2010), in their extensive summary of European policies in this field, noted that as family concerns grew, typologies also shifted from rather straightforward calculations of social spending to Esping-Andersen's (1990) review of the degree to which families were able to maintain a normal standard of living regardless of their market performance, for example, through a suite of protective state benefits. He assessed the relationship between the state, market and family in social provision, and produced a typology that differentiated between liberal, conservative and social democratic welfare regimes. The liberal UK was found to be market-led with high levels of individual responsibility and an emphasis on means testing. Conservative welfare states, such as Germany, had status-preserving social security systems and the promotion of the traditional family at their core. The social democratic states of Scandinavia, on the other hand, offered extensive universal state benefits coupled with a high degree of solidarity and gender equality. This typology laid the foundations to which subsequently refinements were added, with an increased emphasis on governments' family responses.

Matters of gender and the role of families in social provision were given a higher profile in typologies such as the strong, moderate and weak male breadwinner model analysis (Lewis and Ostner, 1994). Esping-Andersen himself introduced a specific family orientation through assessing states' level of 'de-familialisation', that is, 'the degree to which household's welfare and caring responsibilities are relaxed either via welfare state provision or via market provision' (Esping-Andersen, 1999, p 51). Ostner (2003, 2009) further refined this approach through classifying positive and negative de- or re-familialisation. Negative means the constraint of life choices, for example, through a reduction of care services; positive measures do the reverse, for example, through the expansion of care services and the introduction of care allowances.

Another family policy typology analysed the functional expenditure for families as a proportion of total social spending (Schubert et al, 2009). Government expenditure and support received by families form the basis for a number of comparative studies. Gauthier (2002), for example, has examined convergence between European countries in relation to these matters.

Family policy-making styles were the subject of Kamerman and Kahn's (1978) analysis, with an explicit and comprehensive style in evidence in, for example, Sweden, France and Hungary, a sectoral approach in Austria, Germany and Poland, and a reluctant and implicit family policy in the UK. In yet one more model, Gauthier (1996) identified four types of state family policy: pro-egalitarian as in Denmark, pro-family and pro-natalist as in France, pro-traditionalist as in Germany, and pro-family, but not interventionist, offering limited means-tested support, as in the UK. The role of institutions and administrative structures are also analysed in the context of family policy trends in comparative studies such as that undertaken by Hantrais (2004).

FAMILYPLATFORM's comprehensive European-wide analysis of these and other typologies found that many were not able to respond sufficiently to a changing policy environment and shifting clusters of countries (Blum and Rille-Pfeiffer, 2010). Thus, for example, France has an explicit policy with a commitment to support the family in its constitution, in contrast with the de-familial, individualistic and pro-gender equality focus of Nordic countries. And yet, with its pro-natal stance, France has high levels of childcare that equate with those in Scandinavia, and it also has high levels of female employment. A similar trend is now in evidence in Germany. Formerly classified as conservative on family issues and committed to uphold the traditional family and male breadwinner model, Germany has shifted substantially with its moves to assist the reconciliation of work and childcare for women in order to tackle the fertility deficit. Government tolerance and support for different family forms is also breaking through familiar boundaries (for example, in Catholic Spain). In 2007, 13 of the 27 countries in the EU offered civil partnership facilities, and the numbers continue to rise (Boele-Wolki, 2007). The changes in former communist European countries are also difficult to accommodate in transnational analyses. These challenges to formerly stable classifications reflect the growing complexity of socio-political trends. They may be further exacerbated by the economic retrenchment experienced at different levels across Europe, prompting a variety of responses that are not fully played out. The typologies also suffer from an absence of a commonly accepted definition of family policy, and it is significant that often family law, eldercare and the intergenerational dimension across the age span are missing from the indicators. Comparative analyses are frequently confined to single issues, such as work–life balance matters or family supports.

There does appear, then, to be a need to develop a new typology that could accommodate these constantly changing dimensions of family policy and the divergence within and convergence across clusters of countries. In drawing it up there is a critical requirement for a commonly accepted definition of family policy that eschews a narrow focus and embraces support and regulation across the generations including issues associated with family functioning, morality and law; the typology would need to be able to reflect the totality of family policy.

## Family policy in the United Kingdom pre-1997

As we have seen in the European overview, the UK's position through the post-war decades has been to have a fairly low family policy profile. The welfare state existed, albeit at a fairly low level of universal provision. A non-interventionist approach prevailed. There was no radical promotion of gender equality as in Scandinavia, and no emphasis on upholding the traditional family to the degree evinced in some socially conservative countries. Concerns over fertility rates did not emerge, and pro-natalist motives have not informed British policy.

However, family began to have greater purchase towards the end of the Conservative administration in the 1990s under John Major (Appleton and Byrne, 2003). This was a period when there were anxieties over social fragmentation associated with recession and the socio-political upheaval experienced in the UK as it moved from a manufacturing economy with stable, often lifelong employment and linked communities, to a financial service-led economy, de-unionised with unstable employment patterns. One by-product was an endeavour to bolster the role of family. The rhetoric was typified by the slogan of getting 'back to basics'. There was something of a puritanical crusade on issues of sexual morality that backfired on a number of ministers who had strayed from the marital home.

But alongside this public pantomime was a growing interest in family support initiatives, particularly in relation to early years interventions. Parton (2008) has drawn attention to research in the 1990s on early childhood supports and their impact on outcomes. The targeted programmes in the US, with their widely publicised evaluations, gained attention – in particular the Perry Pre-School project with its claim to save government expenditure in the long term because of its impact on children (Schweinhart and Weikart, 1993, 1997). Parenting programmes were explored and developed with a strong social crime prevention motive as anxieties over youth crime and its increase were pervasive (Utting et al, 1993). The Parenting Forum, later to be renamed Parenting UK, was set up by the National Children's Bureau. There were the seeds of interest and development, but what was to follow under the New Labour administration was of a different order of magnitude.

## Family policy since 1997

One of the most radical developments in the scope of government over the last decade has been the shift in the role of the state vis-à-vis personal relationships. The parent–child relationship came centre stage; family and parenting services mushroomed; there were Sure Start children's centres in every locality, parenting service commissioners, strategies, programmes, orders and more. The government sought to improve the way children behave and learn through positively manipulating family relationships. For adults work–life balance provision, and marriage and couple services grew substantially, while in terms of human rights there were civil partnerships and a range of measures around equality in relations. It was a formidable catalogue of social change and a movement in government operations that has not only had an impact in the UK, but has been emulated abroad (Commission on Families and the Wellbeing of Children, 2005; James, 2009; Henricson, 2010).

The process and thinking is documented in a host of strategy documents, ranging from the initial *Supporting families* (Home Office, 1998) to *Every child matters* (HM Treasury, 2003) and its sequels, and culminating during the last year of the New Labour government with plans for widely accessible services in *Support for all* (DCSF, 2010) and *Building Britain's future*, in which the then Prime Minister announced a move 'from a system based primarily on targets and central direction to one where individuals have enforceable entitlements over the service they receive' (Prime Minister, 2009, p 18).

Family policy exemplified the major tenets of New Labour philosophy, and the aspiration was enormous, addressing the whole social fabric. It was not the stuff of restricted family policy, for example, to enhance fertility rates traditionally pursued in some European countries (Cizek and Richter, 2004). Macroeconomic influence was involved, and social enhancement. The aim was to reduce child poverty, increase social mobility and improve child outcomes – breaking the cycle of deprivation – and to deliver social cohesion (Henricson, 2003). There have also been drivers engaged with happiness and wellbeing, endorsing Sen's approach of moving away from assessing income to assessing functions and capabilities (Sen, 1992; Cabinet Office, 2006; Pedace, 2008).

## Questions on the record

... our historic aim that ours is the first generation to end child poverty forever, and it will take a generation. It is a 20-year mission but I believe it can be done. (Blair, 1999, p 7)

The Government is committed to ending child poverty, tackling social exclusion and promoting the welfare of all children so that they can thrive and have the opportunity to fulfil their potential as citizens throughout their lives. There are a number of programmes such as Sure Start, Connexions and Quality Protects and a range of policies to support families, promote educational attainment, reduce truancy and social exclusion and secure a future for all young people in education, employment or training. (DH, 2000a, p x)

Although the achievements during the New Labour government's period in office were wide ranging, there are issues arising over the role accorded family policy and its delivery. The analysis undertaken in this study assesses not only the philosophy, dynamic and social attitudes behind these significant trends in public policy, but also the degree to which the aspirations were met or were indeed realisable. The question is asked as to whether this whole conceptual approach and project of social betterment was appropriate as a point of reference for family policy.

There have been criticisms levelled that the aspirations have not been achieved. Child poverty targets and a major shift in social mobility have proved elusive (OECD, 2008a; Brewer et al, 2009; Hills et al, 2009). There were certainly shortfalls, but arguably the analysis to date has been blinkered by a two-fold process, a simplistic focus on the missing of self-imposed government targets, coupled with an habituation of the progressive agenda. There was perhaps something of the spoilt child scenario – society took the goods for granted and continued to ask for more. Demands were ratcheted up, particularly from civil society that only seemed able to operate in complaining mode.

Less prominence has been given to the charge that the aspirations were simply too extravagant, that it was unrealistic to expect to change a highly unequal society, which the UK is, through supporting personal relationships; and there has been even less discussion of the possibility that the aspirations were too high in respect of changing personal relationships and behaviours. Was there, in effect, at the core of the New Labour narrative too high an expectation of human malleability?

There have also been questions over the emphasis on childhood at the expense of other generations (Henricson and Bainham, 2005). Undoubtedly the aspiration to change social relations – to break the poverty cycle for future generations, through the manipulation of behaviours related to parenting and education – would be likely to result in such a skew. Rhetoric concerned with balancing interests across the generations was not in evidence, and arguably the New Labour government, with its preoccupation with child outcomes, had rather more of a child policy than a family policy to its credit.

With these questions to the fore, this book analyses the New Labour record, and the Coalition government's response. As well as assessing positive and negative impacts, it examines political motivation and the external influences on government thinking, ranging from public opinion and interest groups to international governance and a growing administrative and social homogeneity in Europe.

## Matters for the future

The study then moves on to explore options for the future with a view to the publication acting as a springboard for debate. This prospective part of the discussion has particular reference to a role for public policy in managing human relations in a way that is sufficiently aspirational to be of consequence, while also being realistic and determined by achievable outcomes.

It establishes the parameters and expected returns for family policy replacing the current ill-defined fluidity. With the promotion of family wellbeing framed as the core objective of such a policy, there are recommendations to address the tensions within families, the division between the state and the family's obligation of care across the generations, and splits between the state, family and individual in shaping and regulating moral conduct. A set of coherent support and control policies for family relations are developed which endorse an awareness of the need to manage fundamental tensions in human and family relationships, recognising that while they may be supportive, relationships are also steeped in conflict. The proposals constitute a radical shift in perspective for future progressive governments.

This development of a model for the future is informed by a set of principles that range from an endorsement of human rights to an acknowledgement of the need to promote a transparent and realistic, practical framework. They include recognition of tensions within society and a major role for the state in addressing these. They embrace the need to accommodate separate and common interests in families, and to provide a balanced and complementary set of services across the generations. Overall the values embodied in these principles are humanistic. They do not promote a simple utilitarian standard – the greatest happiness of the majority of family members – but rather one that has as its aim maximising the wellbeing of all.

## The principles

- The purpose of family policy is to promote family wellbeing across genders and across the generations.
- Family policy should support and control family relationships, managing tensions between individuals with particular reference to the duty of the state to safeguard human rights.
- Family policy should manage the relationship between the state and the family, clearly defining their respective caring obligations and promoting social justice for families.
- Within an overarching commitment to human rights, family policy should accommodate shifts in social mores and morality over time and in the context of a multicultural society, combining the need to preserve a level of stability with a responsive approach.
- Family policy should be developed in an international context, with particular reference to Europe in the light of international law and social administration, and increasing levels of labour mobility and migration.
- Family policy should be explicit with a set of clearly defined and achievable goals reflecting these core values.

## Content

The opening chapters of the book analyse family policy over the last 15 years. This analysis then informs the proposals to support family wellbeing through a realignment of the policy paradigm. The discussion takes place in the following sequence of chapters.

Chapter Two, 'The changed landscape', describes the state of family policy in the UK at the departure of the New Labour administration, with a focus on substantial developments where there was some distinctive change in direction or scale of service. On the back of the evidence, two key theme areas emerge – *social liberalism* and *support and control*.

Chapter Three, What was at the root of it?', discusses the philosophy, social attitudes and international influences behind the principal themes to have emerged in family policy. It analyses the philosophical and political discourse, commentaries and attitudinal studies.

Chapter Four, 'The legacy and the Coalition government', considers the response of the current Coalition government to New Labour's support and regulation of family life, including matters of philosophy and approach. The new government's proposals and record after its first year in office are reviewed.

Chapter Five, 'What was wrong?', critiques common and less familiar perceptions of the shortcomings of family policy under the New Labour administration. It assesses the sources, nature and legitimacy of the complaints. A series of questions are posed to elicit points for change. There is reflection on successes and a questioning of perceptions of failure as a result of self-imposed targets. Over-ambitious expectations of behaviour change and the misplaced role of family policy in tackling differences in income and social outcomes are challenged, as is the absence of an holistic family policy balancing interests across the generations.

Chapter Six, 'Looking to the future', moves from the analysis to the proposition, laying the conceptual foundations for developing family policy. It assesses what is realistic and what a purposeful policy would be for a future phase of progressive government. Following an elucidation of the importance of conceptual clarity, there is full discussion of the role of family policy in supporting and regulating family relationships and in determining the relationship between state and family in their caring function. A further role for family policy is explored in providing a responsive interface between socio-legal administration and changes in social mores and morality. The possibility of the proposal giving rise to a new or modified family policy tool of analysis is also mooted.

The core features of this change in approach to families and public policy are drawn together in a concluding chapter, which advocates nine steps towards a new family policy. There is a review of the proposals in relation to political and economic futures, and critically the impact of the proposed reorientation is run against different scenarios of service contraction and growth.

## Nature of the book

This book is a discursive think piece intended to launch a debate on the future of family policy. As such it combines detailed study of the evidence with a radical rethink of future directions. It has been informed by a review of British and European government and intergovernmental documentation which has implications for family policy including legislation, directives, rights conventions, summaries of significant care law, strategies, political speeches and programme planning and evaluation. There has also been consideration of commentaries on family policy and associated theoretical models and developments. The period examined was from 1997 to 2011.

Finally it is important to note that, while the discussion has been substantively drawn from an assessment of this literature, it has also been influenced by the author's experience of some two decades in the family policy field, working closely with government and exchanging thoughts and views with a wide range of national and international experts. This experience has convinced her not only of the worth of the family policy enterprise and of past achievements, but also of the benefits to be had in the future from a fundamental shift in understanding of the role of this pivotal sphere of government.

# TWO

# The changed landscape

This chapter looks at family policy as administered by New Labour. It provides an overview leading to the consideration of influences, motives, failures and options for the future direction of travel in subsequent chapters. The core elements of governmental activity are summarised,[1] and then the principal differences with what went before are drawn out in a section entitled 'So what was different?'. The themes of *social liberalism* and *support and control* inform the discussion.

## Policies

### Social liberalism

Social liberalism in government has been on the increase throughout the 20th and 21st centuries. But it has not increased consistently over time; there have been fits and starts, with two major spurts, one in the 1960s and early 1970s, and the other during the period of the New Labour administration. Principally in relation to family policy, social liberalism is concerned with matters of gender equality and the accommodation of different family formations and ways of living.

#### *Work, care and gender equality*

The growth in social liberalism has been in evidence not only in the UK, but also in Europe, where the thrust of family policy has been particularly concerned with the reconciliation of emergent work patterns as caring and paid employment have become more evenly shared between the sexes. The Council of Europe, for example, focused its review of European family policy on this theme, reflecting the preoccupation of member states (Committee of Experts on Social Policy for Families and Children, 2009).

The UK was part of this movement and now has one of the longest periods of maternity leave in Europe. The incremental array of measures taken by the New Labour government, such as the 2002 Employment Act and the 2006 Work and Families Act, has resulted in maternity pay being available for nine months with the right to additional unpaid leave for up to a year. There were also provisions for transferring paid maternity leave to fathers, which subsequently came to be put into effect by the Coalition government. Unpaid paternity leave had been made available for fathers in 1999 when the government implemented the 1996 European Commission Parental Leave Directive (96/34/EC) as one of its early indications of engagement in this field. The rate of maternity pay also increased, from £59.55 in 1999 to £123.06 in 2009, a substantial increase, albeit not commensurate with median earnings (James, 2009).

Under New Labour accessible extensive provision of childcare was embraced as an essential commodity, with its double benefit of enabling mothers to work and supporting early years development; it was particularly beneficial for disadvantaged families (Commission on Families and the Wellbeing of Children, 2005). From being low in the league table of European states, childcare in the UK was brought into the spotlight with a creditable range of provision in evidence by 2010 (OECD, 2005; Henricson, 2008). The commitment was in evidence from the beginning of the New Labour period in office – the 1998 Childcare Strategy set out: 'to ensure good quality, affordable childcare for children aged 0 to 14 in every neighbourhood' (DfEE, 1998, p 7).

The aim was to raise the quantity and quality of childcare through a process of taxation credits, raising the number of childcare places and extending access. Funding increased substantially over the period, more than doubling between 2003 and 2006. The number of registered childcare places more than doubled between 1997 and 2008 rising to 1.3 million (DCSF, 2009a). The 2006 Childcare Act placed a duty on local authorities to ensure that there were sufficient childcare facilities for working parents in their area, and there was to be a substantial role for Sure Start children's centres and schools in delivery. From 2007 entitlement to 15 hours of free early education places was available for three- and four-year-olds, with a long-term aim of providing 20 hours a week. There were also measures to improve professional standards in childcare with the establishment of a Transformation Fund and new qualifications. This was coupled with a single quality framework for services (James, 2009).

*Family formation*

The liberation of women to work, and in some measure of men to care, was closely entwined with the government's support programme and its aspiration to influence behaviours and social outcomes. In the other strand of New Labour's family policy social liberalism agenda there was rather more of an unadulterated concern to promote individual human rights. A suite of reforms was introduced which eliminated discriminatory treatment of different family forms. These measures were closely connected to the requirements of the Human Rights Act which was introduced by New Labour in 1998.

The first of the measures related to putting non-married couples and single adults on the same financial footing vis-à-vis the state as married couples. If support was to be provided for children, it was to be done irrespective of the marital status of their parents. The married couple's tax allowance was consequently abolished in 2000.

Marriage was also no longer to be a pre-requisite for fertility treatment or adoption. The 2007 Adoption and Children Act enabled single people and unmarried couples to adopt. The Act further provided that unmarried fathers, on registering the birth of a child with the mother, would also acquire 'parental responsibility'.

In 1997 discrimination against homosexuality and same-sex couples was still an integral part of family law. Its redress was one of New Labour's most notable human rights achievements. The

Civil Partnership Act was passed in 2005 giving same-sex couples the facility of being able to register their partnerships and thereby accrue the same rights and responsibilities that they would have done had they entered civil marriage. The Equality (Sexual Orientation) Regulations came into effect in 2007 prohibiting sexual orientation discrimination in the provision of goods and services. In the family sphere this prevented discrimination against same-sex couples should they wish to adopt a child.

In terms of fertilisation treatment, the position of adults and same-sex partners was further protected under the 2008 Human Fertilisation and Embryology Act which removed the obligation of clinics to consider the need for a father, replacing the term 'father' with 'supportive parenting'. Furthermore, both same-sex partners were to now have the right to be named on a child's birth certificate (James, 2009).

The breadth of this range of examples of social liberalism is considerable. There may have been hopes for further measures, such as the introduction of civil partnership facilities for cohabitees, and even the relaxation of the law on assisted dying. Nevertheless, the progressive liberal shift is demonstrable, and together with the introduction of that fundamental measure affecting human relations, the 1998 Human Rights Act, it is a substantial record that is a worthy successor of the reforms of the Labour administrations of the 1960s and 1970s which saw the introduction of equal opportunities and anti-discrimination legislation, and the legalisation of homosexuality and abortion.

## Support and control

The scope of New Labour's support and control measures was at least commensurate, if not more formidable than this social liberalism wing of its endeavour. The array of initiatives was sufficient to elicit comment in international analytical studies, and indeed some of the measures prompted emulation abroad (Henricson, 2010). It should be noted, however, that it was support for parents and children in the context of their families that was the predominant theme. Care for older people, while in evidence, was of less moment.

*Financial support to help 'hard working families'*

Child wellbeing was supported by a host of fiscal measures to reduce child poverty and to support the financial viability of families in bringing up children. Tax credits were a significant feature of the system that was introduced. The final form that the credits took as of 2003 was the Working Tax Credit and the Child Tax Credit. The former was a credit for low-paid workers with a childcare element allowing families to claim for 80 per cent of childcare costs. The latter, the Child Tax Credit, provided support to the main carer in or out of work. It was paid in full up to a certain threshold of income and then gradually reduced. Some 90 per cent of families were entitled to all or part of this, with a further child element reserved for lower-income families only – approximately 50 per cent of families (Brewer, 2003; James, 2009).

Alongside this escalation of means-related support, universal child benefit remained, and following a hike in 1999 for the first child, rose in line with inflation (Bennett and Dornan, 2006). This contrasted with periods in the 1980s when child benefit had not been up-rated at all so that child benefit in 1997 was 'worth less in real terms than in 1979, even though average earnings had increased in real terms by around 50% during that period' (Commission on Families and the Wellbeing of Children, 2005, p 75).

The Sure Start Maternity Grant doubled, and over time quadrupled the amount pregnant mothers received, albeit with a proviso that professional health advice should be obtained. A further Health in Pregnancy Grant was available to those who took up an antenatal care offer.

The Child Trust Fund was a further innovatory universal entitlement with each child receiving a £250 voucher for investment, with access deferred until they were 18 years of age. Interest from the voucher and contributions to the fund made by family and friends was tax-free. Double the amount was available to children from low-income families, and various other additions were subsequently made.

The crusade to reduce child poverty was central to the New Labour mission, and latterly as re-election became less likely, steps were taken to try and ensure that the work would continue. The Child Poverty Act was passed in 2010 requiring the Secretary of State to meet child poverty reduction targets, and to continue with strategic development reporting regularly on progress.

### Services

The legacy on child poverty was complemented in the field of family services. There was major investment in a variety of measures to support children's upbringing, from early home learning to adult couple relationships.

Sure Start is perhaps the most memorable of New Labour's initiatives and in which it is perhaps seen in its most positive light. The aim of the programme was – and is – to promote the physical, intellectual and social development of babies and young children so that they can flourish at home and when they get to school, thereby breaking the cycle of disadvantage for new generations of young children. The core of the programme offered included a visit to all new parents introducing them to Sure Start services, enhanced childcare, play and learning opportunities, better access to both child and maternal health services and a range of parenting courses and groups. Sure Start was initially located in areas of acute deprivation, but within those areas the offer was universal for all parents.

Over New Labour's term in office Sure Start was expanded until by 2004 there were some 3,000 centres across the country reaching every locality (DCSF, 2009b). It was a national universal service with more intensive provision, including additional outreach work, provided in disadvantaged areas.

There was also a strategic approach to supporting parents that went considerably beyond Sure Start. A service network was established which encompassed investment in innovative voluntary sector approaches through to detailed planning requirements of local authorities. The following are some examples (James, 2009):

- The Parenting Fund was created providing direct central government finance to the voluntary sector in developing best practice parenting initiatives, with a particular focus on marginalised groups whose needs were not being met by mainstream services.

- Alongside children's centres, schools became 'extended', offering not only pre- and post-school hours childcare facilities, but also hubs providing parenting support activities, a fast route to targeted and specialist services and adult and family learning opportunities.

- Parent support advisers were established in some 10-15 schools in each local authority area, offering advice and help to parents in need of particular support. Expert parent advisers with a particular focus on anti-social behaviour were also made available.

- Other targeted support relating to families and responding to concerns over families at risk and anti-social behaviour included Family Nurse Partnerships and Family Intervention Projects. These programmes adopted an intensive whole family approach. *Think family: Improving the life chances of families at risk* (Social Exclusion Task Force, 2008) provided strategic policy guidance to working with the family as a unit.

- On the planning and delivery front, local authorities were expected to develop a parenting strategy and to offer a suite of services through from early universal services to targeted and intensive responses. In an endeavour to improve investment decisions in this field following an evidence-based approach, local authorities were required to appoint a single commissioner of parenting support services, and a toolkit of the evidence pertinent to different programmes was provided. Local authorities were also required to have a parents' champion as a policy and practice advocate.

New Labour's activities in supporting adult couple relationships developed in response to a widespread recognition of the impact of parents' relationships on their children's outcomes. Following Sir Graham Hart's review advocating public investment (Hart, 1999), the Marriage and Relationship Support Grant was established, which was subsequently absorbed into the Children, Young People and Families Grant. This funding was further augmented by the Department for Children, Schools and Families in 2008 when, in addition to funding organisations delivering relationship support, pilots were set in train to improve the coordination of support for separating couples. The national Children's Plan (DCSF, 2007) provided that Sure Start outreach staff should support adult couple relationships after the birth of a child, and health visitors were given similar functions by the Department of Health (James, 2009).

The incremental delivery of this array of family services required national and local strategic development. Strategies and planning documents abounded, some of which had an overarching function. Of these, *Every child matters* (HM Treasury, 2003), with its various follow-up documents such as *Every parent matters* (DfES, 2007), was perhaps the most significant. Starting from the broad five aims for children of being healthy, staying safe, enjoying and achieving, making a positive contribution and experiencing economic wellbeing, the strategy and its derivatives go on to provide detailed processes for delivery. Included in these was the establishment by the 2004 Children Act of multiagency children's trusts and requirements for Children and Young People's Plans for the delivery of cohesive children's services at the local level. Planning at a national level was also drawn together with the Department of Health's children's social services functions moving to the then Department for Education and Skills, and the latter eventually having an overarching family policy function as the renamed Department for Children, Schools and Families.

## Controls

Support and control frequently dovetail, not least because the intent behind support is often to manipulate behaviour, albeit in a benign and relatively gentle fashion. Some support interventions like the Family Intervention Projects go beyond this and combine overt control, such as a requirement that families agree to a contract of behaviour, alongside an offer of assistance. Here we look at examples of overt control introduced by New Labour.

## Criminal justice

The use of control is particularly in evidence in the criminal justice field, the prime example being the Parenting Order. Brought in by the 1998 Crime and Disorder Act, and expanded by the 2003 Anti-Social Behaviour Act, the Parenting Order gave magistrates the opportunity, where a child had committed an offence or had truanted, of directing the parent to engage in some form of guidance or counselling. It also enabled requirements to be placed on the parent to exercise control over the child. The Anti-Social Behaviour Act further introduced the Parenting Contract for use where a child had been excluded from school for disciplinary reasons, or had regularly truanted requiring the parent to comply with certain actions designed to improve the child's conduct. Under the *Respect action plan* (Home Office, 2006), the arrangements for Parenting Orders were again expanded, enabling them to be imposed for serious misbehaviour in school even if the child had not been excluded. Furthermore, schools and other agencies, such as community safety and housing officers, were now able to make direct applications for Parenting Orders and Parenting Contracts. On a less formal footing, school contracts became commonplace during this period, with requirements placed on the parents of all children in a school with regard to time keeping, homework supervision, behaviour control and the like.

## Conditionality

Behavioural manipulation was also in evidence in the economic sphere. As we have seen, some benefits, specifically maternity benefits, were made conditional on obtaining health and parenting advice. Other conditional measures related to work behaviours. As part of the drive to reduce child poverty steps were taken to encourage single parents into work, while balancing their childcare responsibilities. Following the New Deal for Lone Parents offering voluntary advice on job seeking, training, benefits and childcare, the government moved towards a compulsory approach. In 2001 compulsory annual Work-Focused Interviews were introduced. By 2010 under the Welfare Reform Act of that year, single parents and partners of Jobseeker's Allowance claimants whose youngest child was aged one to seven were placed in a 'progression to work' category. Where the youngest child was seven or over they were classified as 'work ready'. The latter had job search requirements, and faced benefit sanctions for non-attendance at job centres or participation in work-related activities (James, 2009).

## Child protection

The child protection controls introduced during this era exemplify a rather different aspect of control, one of increasing levels of surveillance and detection. Anxieties over serious incidents of child abuse had resulted in enquiries and associated recommendations for the enhancement of coordination between agencies (Laming, 2003). The government introduced a group of measures to meet these requirements. As well as the multiagency teams providing support through children's centres and extended schools, a Common Assessment Framework was adopted applicable to all services working with children. The information recorded would follow the child. With a common approach to assessment, it would improve information sharing and coordination. A national database, ContactPoint, was also established containing basic information in respect of the child –

the contact details of the parents, carers and professionals involved and whether an assessment had been undertaken.

## The older population

What of intergenerational familial dependency other than the axis associated with children's upbringing? There was certainly some enhanced provision for the older population. Pensioner poverty was an issue of concern that New Labour took measures to address. Gordon Brown, the then Chancellor of the Exchequer, pledged at a Labour Party conference to 'end pensioner poverty in our country' (Brown, 2002). There were large increases in means-tested benefits and the Minimum Income Guarantee for the over-60s was introduced with a commitment for it to rise in line with earnings. There were also smaller real increases in non-means-tested benefits including the state pension and winter fuel payments (Goodman et al, 2003).

On the social care front spending was not commensurate with these increases in financial support. Age UK (2011a) noted that between 2004 and 2011 net spending on older people's social care rose by 0.1 per cent in real terms, while there had been a substantial increase in expenditure on the National Health Service (NHS). The funding of social care became a major issue during the New Labour period in office, and a range of reports and consultations on future options were conducted. The Royal Commission on Long-Term Care reported in 1999, and proposals for direct payments and standard safeguards were adopted with the establishment of the National Care Standards Commission. However, the recommendation to make free personal care universally available was not adopted (DH, 2000b). Latterly New Labour became rather more radical, with a proposal to set up a national care service in the White Paper *Building the national care service* (HM Government, 2010a). The proposal opted for comprehensive funding arrangements with the population contributing to a pool according to their means and receiving care free at the point of delivery. The precise method of operation was to be defined, but the election intervened so that no further progress was made.

## So what was different?

All governments take measures and pass laws, if only for self-affirmation and to justify their call on the public purse. The question being asked here is not whether there was activity, but rather whether there was a significant change in kind in the sort of family policy being pursued. Of course such change would have been trailed and been the subject of discourse, research and public debate prior to its promotion by government; the intellectual ground was well prepared before New Labour took office. It would also have been impossible for there to have been no precedents or steps taken on which to build. It is a question of degree, concept and direction of travel – not an expectation of total rebirth.

### Support and control

#### Reduction in child poverty

New Labour's financial support activities in relation to families with children had a significant impact in reversing a trend of increasing child poverty levels in the 1980s and early 1990s. The Commission on Families and the Wellbeing of Children (2005), in its consideration of the levels of poverty that New Labour inherited, found a marked rise from 1979, with the rate of increase tapering and then moving into decline under New Labour.

The Department for Work and Pensions, in its analysis of *Households Below Average Income* (2011), found that relative child poverty declined between 1998/99 and 2009/10 by 6 per cent before housing costs were taken into account, and 5 per cent after housing costs were taken into account; in terms of absolute poverty, the reduction was 15 and 16 per cent respectively.

After 2005 the rate of decline decreased, in part attributable to the escalation of incomes at the top of the scale increasing inequality and depressing calculations of relative poverty levels. Slower economic growth also contributed to a slowing down of the rate at which child poverty was being reduced. As pressure on public spending mounted, the redistribution momentum in the tax and benefit system became less evident (Hills et al, 2009). Nevertheless Hills et al, in their review of poverty and inequality over the entire period of the New Labour administration, concluded that the child poverty reduction record was creditworthy:

> A clearer comparison can be made between the distributional impact of the 2008/09 tax and benefit system and results if the 1996/97 system had been preserved. If, as was the general policy before 1997, benefit levels and tax allowances had been increased in line with price inflation, income inequality and poverty rates would both have been significantly higher than they actually were by 2006/07....
>
> Overall poverty rates would have been 6–7 percentage points higher than the actual outcome, corresponding to a rise in poverty of 4–5 points over the period, rather than the actual fall of 1–3 points by 2006/07. Rather than falling, the child poverty rate would have risen by 6–9 points and the pensioner poverty rate by 7 points. (Hills et al, 2009, p 2)

The decline in child poverty was partly due to economic growth, but, as we have seen, analysts have found that government activity in relation to tax and benefits also had a significant impact:

> The Institute of Fiscal Studies has shown that, since 1999, support for families with children has grown by 52% in real terms (Adam and Brewer, 2004), and it is broadly acknowledged in academic analysis that the government has had significant success in reducing

child poverty, defined in relative as well as absolute terms....(Commission on Families and the Wellbeing of Children, 2005, p 59)

### Parenting support

Parenting support was a creature of the New Labour era. The word itself had been newly coined – being the activity of bringing up children. Formerly a person was a parent, with the noun denoting a status rather than the doing of a job.

There was a substantive discourse on parenting in the 1990s with, for example, the publication of *Confident parents, confident children* (Pugh et al, 1994) and the advocacy of parenting programmes following their development and evaluation in Australia and the US (Henricson and Roker, 2000). There were a range of humanitarian and behavioural approaches under discussion. Behavioural models were distinctly associated with conduct modification, and evaluations found them to be more effective than other models in changing children's behaviour (Patterson, 1994; Henricson and Roker, 2000). These behavioural approaches were coincidentally appropriate tools for a government concerned to enhance pro-social and positive learning behaviours among the young.

The distinctiveness of the New Labour project was to establish a population-wide parenting support network where one had not existed. From parenting programmes to early home learning supports, the move was radical. While advice to parents and family support had been provided through social workers as part of their safeguarding function, this population-wide behaviour modification project was different in scale and kind. Family centres had offered a range of counselling and support services, but these centres were limited in number and targeted at vulnerable families with child protection issues. The Sure Start children's centres were offered as a universal facility. Childcare had, of course, pre-dated New Labour, but the scale of provision, the introduction of free and subsidised access and the breadth of access in terms of location – in schools pre- and post-school hours and in children's centres – were all new.

## Child protection

Of the support and control activities, child protection, within a narrow reactive definition, is perhaps the area of family policy exemplifying least change. The 1980s and early 1990s saw considerable emphasis on child protection investigation within the framework of 'children at risk' and 'children in need' established by the 1989 Children Act (Henricson et al, 2001), and this framework is still in place. The additions of sophisticated database systems and national monitoring and assessment were principally procedural matters designed to enhance the efficient delivery of child protection services. The intention and general approach remained as it had been in previous decades.

The change of direction that was significant for child protection was not peculiar to that area of family policy, but was rather a phenomenon of more general public service reform in favour of tighter specification of service delivery, including target setting and detailed procedural requirements determined by national government departments. In child protection it resulted in a move from motivated professional-oriented decision making with a substantial degree of flexibility and consequent risk, to a system of checks and closely monitored management accountability. Lord Laming, reporting on the 'Baby P' child abuse case, was witness to this change in working methods: 'the tradition of deliberate, reflective social work practice is being put in danger because of an overemphasis on process and targets' (Laming, 2009, p 32).

Other critics have been more vociferous:

> We have argued that all the changes over the past 15 years have led towards increased bureaucracy and regulation, and that this has been a dead end. If there is to be change it must get us out of the blind alley of checklist practice and into authoritative

professionalism which involves trust between the public, professionals and policy makers. (Cooper et al, 2003, p 87)

The new approach to public service administration that had started under Margaret Thatcher's Conservative administration, and which was then continued by New Labour, had its impact on child protection just as it did in other quarters of the public sector (Henricson, 2007).

### Criminal justice

On the criminal justice control front there were some legal and quasi-legal shifts of considerable magnitude sufficient to constitute something of a new relationship between the state and families. Legal expectations of behavioural responsibility took communal norms to a higher level of social control.

The 1998 Crime and Disorder Act and the 2003 Anti-Social Behaviour Act between them reinforced parental responsibility through a process of considerable intervention including, as they did, the requirement to engage with parenting programmes and counselling through Parenting Orders. Not only did this constitute intervention in the intimate precincts of family life, it involved the attribution of dual responsibility for a crime – the child above the age of criminal responsibility (currently set at 10 years) who has committed an offence and the parent. There were precedents for enforcing parental responsibility. For example, the 1933 Children and Young Person's Act enabled courts to require parents to pay financial penalties imposed on their children. And the 1982 Criminal Justice Act introduced a presumption that courts should bind over the parents of a child under the age of 16 and convicted of an offence to 'take proper care of him and exercise proper control over him' (Nacro, 2004). The scope of provisions relating to parents had, however, expanded substantially under New Labour, sufficient for the Commission on Families and the Wellbeing of Children to comment:

These developments signify a far reaching shift in the nature of criminal responsibility. They rest on a justification that amounts, despite the disclaimer in the White Paper, to a presumption of dual responsibility for the offending behaviour of children up to the age of 16. This presumption is based on an interpretation of parental duties for the care and control of children that now includes crime prevention. (Commission on Families and the Wellbeing of Children, 2005, pp 62/63)

The Commission expressed concern that the distinction between parents' duty of care and responsibility for conduct had been blurred with parents having been in effect criminalised for the actions of their children. Anti-Social Behaviour Orders (ASBOs) also extended criminal sanctions beyond crime to anti-social behaviour.

In addition to Parenting Orders that could be imposed in respect of a child's criminal behaviour, there was the issue of contracts. The web of quasi-legal contracts ranging from home school agreements to contracts that could be imposed under the 2003 Anti-Social Behaviour Act following exclusion or disciplinary problems in school all typified an extension of parental responsibility and, certainly in the case of the latter, an expansion of judicial sanctions relating to the role of parenthood.

### Conditionality

Control through government fiscal measures and the attachment of conditions to the receipt of benefits and tax concessions was certainly not new; indeed it is integral to the operation of the system. What was different under New Labour was the nature and purpose of the conditions being imposed. Benefits associated with unemployment had always had conditions attached to them in relation to seeking for work, and these had been tightened over previous decades to address anxieties over the work-shy claiming benefits and with a view to reducing the benefit bill.

The difference under New Labour in terms of family policy was the introduction of conditions designed to influence behaviour that would impact on children's outcomes. Thus we have the requirements to attend clinics and to receive health and childcare advice in relation to maternity grants. We also have the driver of child poverty reduction in the conditions placed on lone parents and the partners of claimants in relation to seeking and readiness for work. The adult worker model in contrast to the male breadwinner model was receiving more than a nudge with the aim of reducing social exclusion.

We do, of course, have the precedent under previous administrations of seeking to influence family relationships in the married couple's allowance. In the interest of providing consistent support for children in all family types, the allowance was abolished under New Labour in one of its socially liberal measures. The direction of travel was rather to provide adult couple relationship support services regardless of marital status, with children's outcomes operating as the key motivating factor.

What can be said, then, of conditionality is that it was not new. Rather conditionality is something of a litmus test of a government's core purpose; and in terms of core purpose, what New Labour had to offer was new.

### The older population

For older people the introduction of a new benefit, the Minimum Income Guarantee, its up-rating in line with earnings and increases in the level of the state pension resulted in a reduction in pensioner poverty (Hills et al, 2009). Pensioner poverty declined between 1998/99 and 2009/10 by 8 per cent before housing costs were taken into account and 13 per cent after housing costs were taken into account; in terms of absolute poverty, the reduction was 17 and 21 per cent respectively (DWP, 2011).

In relation to social care for older people, progress was less evident. While measures were taken to improve standards following the recommendations of the 1999 Royal Commission on Long-Term Care, the problematic funding arrangements for elder care were not addressed until the end of New Labour's time in office. By then it was too late to implement a set of radical proposals for comprehensive cover for the older population. This is in contrast to Scotland, where free personal care was introduced by the Scottish government in accordance with the recommendation of the Royal Commission under the 2002 Community Care and Health (Scotland) Act. The tardiness in England was perhaps indicative that elder care was less of a strategic priority area than the enhancement of child outcomes.

## Social liberalism

And what can be said of social liberalism beyond the cutting of the married couple's allowance? The 1998 Human Rights Act has had an impact on a host of family policy issues such as non-discriminatory treatment of different family forms. The requirement to adhere to human rights had of course pre-dated the Act, and in terms of legal imperative dates back to the 1950 European Convention on Human Rights introduced after the Second World War and enforceable through the European Court of Human Rights. The introduction of domestic legislation, and the ethos and thinking behind it, nevertheless saw a shift in gear in favour of a more socially equitable liberal approach to the regulation of human relationships. The last similar spate of legislation favouring non-discriminatory behaviours and the enhancement of tolerance towards different sorts of family relationships took place under the Labour administrations of the 1960s and 1970s when, inter alia, the following socially liberal acts made their way onto the statute book – the 1970 Equal Pay Act, the 1975 Sex Discrimination Act establishing the Equal Opportunities Commission, the 1967 Abortion Act providing a legal defence to abortion and the 1967 Sexual Offences Act which legalised homosexual acts. Since that time, prior to New Labour, there was no significant progress in this socially liberal sphere of family policy.

Work–life balance had been given a more recent profile in government activity in the 1980s, but the UK had lagged behind other European countries (Lewis, 1992; OECD, 2007). Childcare was viewed as a private affair under Margaret Thatcher's administration, with little government subsidy. The momentum of the drive to facilitate women's role in the workplace gathered considerable pace under New Labour, supporting a shift in work–home relationships sufficient to see a substantial increase in female employment and to give the role of fathers and fatherhood a distinctly higher profile than it had in 1997. While equality across the gender work–care divide may still prove elusive, the dual earner relationship model became firmly entrenched during this decade (Pascall, 2006; Daly, 2011).

## Overview

In summary, by the time New Labour left office, family policy had changed from a relatively insubstantial function of government in the 1980s to one of the most substantial. While child protection had received considerable attention in the early 1990s, the broader body of families and parents had not. The push by New Labour to change parenting behaviour at a population-wide level was new and altered the relationship between the state and the family, with the former taking a more active role in supporting the upbringing of the nation's children. The change was of sufficient moment to merit international attention and emulation. It was described as the most advanced and comprehensive national parenting support programme in Europe in an international comparative conference held at the University of New South Wales, Australia (Katz and Levine, 2010).

Similar advances had not been made in respect of those aspects of family support that relate to the elderly population. While there was an increase in financial support to pensioners, relatively little progress was made in addressing the pressures and inequalities in elder care. The focus of government attention appeared to be biased towards the younger generation, and family policy was not integrated across the generations.

As well as there being unprecedented support with childrearing, the UK, in 2010, was a more socially liberal place than it had been in 1997. Different family formations had official recognition and greater protection, and there was greater equality between women and men across the work–care divide. Human rights had become part of the family policy profile in a way that they had not been in the 1980s and 1990s.

In sum, New Labour had ushered in progressive family policy with major aspirations. In the next chapter we examine what lay behind this social change.

**Note**

[1] For a detailed resume of policy see James (2009).

# THREE

# What was at the root of it?

It is important to understand the perceptions and trends of thought that informed these changes and continuities in New Labour's family policy. What made family policy tick? Where did the momentum come from for its multiple directions, and how far did these prompts and influences contradict or complement each other? We need this understanding not only to be able to assess the achievements and failures of the New Labour decade, but also, and perhaps more significantly at this juncture, when a new phase in politics is being embarked on, to ground debate in an appreciation of the social forces with which family policy needs to engage. In this chapter there is a discussion of the philosophy and social attitudes behind the principal themes to have emerged, and there is an analysis of the philosophical and political discourse and attitudinal studies.

## Social liberalism

The *social liberalism* theme has been substantially determined independently of government. Post-war social liberation has escalated through the decades and has done so largely despite the stance of different governments. While there have been fits and starts, there is no significant evidence of regression to less liberal attitudes. Indeed trends towards cohabitation and single parenthood have continued through epochs of financial support for marriage and other measures to make single parenthood a less attractive option. Haskey (2001) has described trends in post-war Western Europe across extra-marital sex, marriage, cohabitation and family structure as a fundamental change in demographic and associated social norms. Duncan and Phillips (2008) have spoken of a movement from relational social aims to a focus on individual self-fulfilment and personal development. There has been a process of 'individualisation' and 'detraditionalisation' that has arisen in the context of growing prosperity, welfare and universal education (Beck, 1992; Hunt, 2009). Let us first look at some of the actual shifts in behaviour, and then at what surveys of attitudes reveal, as reviewed in *Family trends* (Hunt, 2009).

The number of extra-marital births has shown an extraordinary rise in the post-war years. In the UK in 1951 4.2 per cent of births were extra-marital. The figure rose to 38 per cent by 1998 and 45 per cent by 2008 (Hunt, 2009). Eurostat (2009) figures show a similar steady increase across Europe during the period of the New Labour administration, 1997-2007. In terms of marriage, although there is some fluctuation, the trend is significantly downwards. First marriages in the UK dropped by almost 10 per cent between 1976 and 2006 (ONS, 2008).

The British Social Attitudes Survey has surveyed attitudes to sexual and associated social behaviour since the early 1980s. Questions on views of pre-marital sex demonstrate a significant increase in tolerance in this area with implications for cohabitation (Duncan and Phillips, 2008). There is also growing tolerance of couples having children outside marriage, with respondents agreeing with the proposition, 'People who want children ought to get married', dropping from 70 per cent in 1989 to 54 per cent in 2000 (Barlow et al, 2001).

Comparisons between marriage and cohabitation were undertaken in the British Social Attitudes Survey 2006, showing high levels of tolerance, with 66 per cent agreeing with the proposition that 'There is little difference between being married and living together', compared with 19 per cent disagreeing (Duncan and Phillips, 2008). The survey also found that divorce had become normalised in attitudes, with 63 per cent agreeing with the proposition that 'Divorce can be a positive first step towards a new life', compared with 7 per cent disagreeing (Barlow et al, 2008).

The introduction of civil partnerships for same-sex couples constituted one of the most radical of the New Labour government's socially liberal initiatives, going to the heart of possible prejudice. However, the indications are that the tolerance demonstrated over pre-marital sex and cohabitation was also developing in relation to homosexuality. The British Social Attitudes Survey 2006 found that 58 per cent agreed that 'Civil partnerships should have the same rights as married couples', and 60 per cent supported the statement that 'A same sex couple can be just as committed to each other as a man and a woman' (Duncan and Phillips, 2008).

Social liberalism has partly been propelled by the reality of practical living. Thus there have been economic imperatives behind the growing numbers of women taking up paid employment through the childbearing years. Dex (2003) has described the economic factors that have supported the increasing equality of women in the workplace, in particular the decline in men's relative income and periods of recession that depressed male employment in the 1990s. Aspirations for self-fulfilment and independence have also featured as a significant motive (Hinds and Jarvis, 2000). Growing convergence between sexual roles and expectations has been a significant feature in social attitudes of the last decade, and this is reflected in governmental measures to facilitate women's participation in the workplace and men's increased engagement with caring and the life of their children. Indeed *Social justice: Strategies for national renewal* (Commission on Social Justice, 1994), which informed New Labour's early strategy, described the changes to the position of women in employment and at home as a social revolution to which the then Conservative government had responded inadequately. Help for women and men in realising these changed roles and in increasing their self-fulfilment became one of the core features of the Commission's proposals across the work–family interface.

Social attitudes are persuasive to governments of any hue, and failure to take cognisance of them is a political hazard. Indeed the datedness of the Conservative government's attitudes to sexual behaviour with censure of private lives was one, if not the principal cause, of its poor showing in the polls in 1997. New Labour had a keener awareness of the social mood when it complained of: 'moral authoritarianism represented by the 1988 Local Government Act and its ban on the "teaching" of "pretended" (gay and lesbian) family relationships' (Commission on Social Justice, 1994, p 312). It is noteworthy that David Cameron, when he spoke on the steps of Number 10 in his prime ministerial acceptance speech, said that the achievement of the New Labour administration had been to create a more open society (Cameron, 2010).

But population-wide attitudes are not the only influences. There is a complicated dynamic between the groundswell of opinion, the vociferous arguments of lobby groups and international pressures. Marrying these pressures with government's own ideological grounding is the stuff of politics and well exemplified in the socially liberal theme of New Labour's family policy record. Here we look at a range of examples with rather different lead influences in this process.

## The melee of influences in the direction of social liberalism: three examples

### Work–life balance

Work–life balance has already been alluded to in the analysis of public attitudes supporting gender equality and a movement towards a more flexible approach to paid labour and caring responsibilities. De facto public behaviour determined the direction of government here, but with other supporting influences. The participation of women in paid work was viewed as one of the key ways of taking families and children out of poverty. The government believed that the most likely way in which impoverished parents would be able to improve their and their children's prospects was by gaining a foothold in the world of work. In order to achieve this goal it sought to ensure that work paid through measures such as the Working Tax Credit with its attendant childcare allowances. It also sought to encourage return to work by lone parents through the New Deal arrangements. More generally, the government made a substantial commitment to increasing the availability of childcare to help parents, mothers in particular, to take up paid work. Its actions supported maximising income through the 'the adult worker' model (Lewis and Giullari, 2005), where both men and women worked in paid employment and children were cared for in formal care settings.

> But we also believe that work is the best form of welfare and our aim is to help people into work and up the earnings ladder. We must move away from merely compensating people for their poverty through the benefits system. We are helping all adults, including parents back to work through the New Deal....
>
> We are leading the way in creating a family friendly tax system. We are not only using the benefits system to help families with children, but using the tax system, helping families into work and ensuring that work pays. (Brown, 1999, p 9)

The push from public attitudes synchronised well with this core governmental goal of poverty reduction. Further leverage came from the EU with its forceful advocacy of progressive work–life balance policies. One of the earliest moves by the New Labour administration was to implement the 1996 EC Parental Leave Directive (96/34/EC) and the 1997 EC Part-Time Work Directive. This EU momentum was motivated by pressures to increase the ease of labour mobility and by concerns over a declining fertility rate in a number of countries which needed to be boosted by supporting working women to have children. Analysis by the FAMILYPLATFORM European research consortium also suggests that the very drawing together of leading bureaucrats and lobby groups engaged with the feminist movement of the 1990s in something of an international hot house had a role to play in taking member states further down the road of supporting mothers' employability and childcare targets than they might otherwise have gone (Ostner, 2010).

### Children's rights

A rather different picture emerges in relation to children's rights. Children's rights did not feature significantly as part of the proposals and discourse of New Labour in opposition. For example, they received scant reference in the report of the Commission on Social Justice (1994) where the focus was on family wellbeing and parenting. The 1997 Labour manifesto made a commitment to introduce the Human Rights Act, but there was no reference to children's rights; the focus again was on family and parenting (Labour Party, 1997).

Neither was there an evident push from public opinion. Children's welfare was supported. There was evidence of changes in adult–child relationships with negotiation between generations replacing rather more authoritarian approaches (Coleman, 1997; Henricson, 2001). However, a rights framework and aspiration was yet to emerge, and there is still no evidence of engagement with this perspective by the public.

The principal drive did not come from public opinion, nor did it come from internal political positioning from within the government, but rather from pressure groups – combined with incentive from international norms. During the early period of the New Labour administration there was a sustained campaign from children's charities and lobby groups such as the Children's Rights Alliance for England to follow precedents in Scandinavia and to appoint a children's commissioner. The United Nations Committee on the Rights of the Child (UNCRC) expressed its concerns over a failure to adopt a rights framework in the following terms: '... the Committee remains concerned at the lack of a rights-based approach to policy development and that the Convention has not been recognised as the appropriate framework for the development of strategies at all levels of the government throughout the State party' (UNCRC, 2002, p 4).

The UNCRC called for the establishment of a children's commissioner in England, and, following the creation of commissioners in Scotland and Wales, the government established the function in the 2004 Children Act. Concession to pressure rather than conviction can be seen here, as New Labour took its time, and, when it acceded to such an office, the terms of reference fell short of rights advocacy. A lesser child welfare promotional position was created – the role does not have a judicial function and is unable, independently of a request from the Secretary of State, to conduct an inquiry into individual complaints (Henricson and Bainham, 2005).

In relation to the curtailment of smacking, the pressure from the children's sector dragged a decidedly reluctant administration. Prior to the passage of the 2004 Children Act, the law provided that evidence of reasonable chastisement could be used as a defence by parents should they assault their child. This old common law defence was challenged in international fora for its contravention of human rights. In 1995 the UNCRC had made a formal recommendation that the British government prohibit corporal punishment. It considered that the defence of reasonable chastisement was open to subjective and arbitrary interpretation and should be removed. In response, government consultations were held on two occasions with the children's sector strongly supportive of a smacking ban. Following these, a change to the legislation was finally introduced, but even then it did not fully comply with the UN's requirement. Although amended by the 2004 Children Act in relation to assault that occasions 'actual bodily harm', the defence of reasonable chastisement is still intact in relation to the lesser offence of 'common assault' (Commission on Families and the Wellbeing of Children, 2005).

What was the cause of this tardiness? Certainly child protection was a government priority, but there was a social control countervailing influence. And more potent than this was the fear that public opinion would be resistant to parental authority being curtailed in this way. Nevertheless, the combined influences of international law, precedents in Scandinavia and a vociferous, relentless lobby from the children's organisations took the government a long way from its original position.

### Family formation

As we have seen, public attitudes to same-sex couple unions were largely tolerant of different family formations. And there were other influences favouring a socially liberal approach. They included precedents from Europe and the government's own engagement with human rights, as evidenced by the introduction of the 1998 Human Rights Act. There was also an historical perspective, with the establishment of the equalities commissions and the legalisation of homosexuality by a previous Labour government. This combination fuelled the introduction of civil partnerships. Interestingly, in relation to family formation, New Labour was prepared, in following the logic of its position, to go beyond public opinion and to allow same-sex couples to adopt children. The British Public Attitudes Survey 2006 showed that public opinion was not supportive of this stance: only 36 per cent agreed with the statement that: 'A lesbian couple are just as capable of being good parents as a man and a woman', and only 31 per cent agreed that a male or gay couple are just as capable of being good parents (Duncan and Phillips, 2008). Possibly the government considered that, as adoption issues apply to only a small portion of the population, it was unlikely to become a highly contentious area – although opposition from the Catholic churches' adoption agencies was vocal (*Christian Today*, 2007).

### Human rights context

We have seen in this theme of social liberalism a common thread of human rights and this was undoubtedly a pervasive motif in the discourse of the period and requires some exploration. A large body of literature was produced and human rights constituted their own academic discipline. Some high profile statutory and voluntary organisations were devoted to their promotion. Human rights provided a bedrock of values against which any public administrative measure could be assessed. The rulings of the European Court of Human Rights had an impact across a wide socio-political landscape, from the right to a family life, to freedom from inhuman and degrading treatment, to preventing discrimination and beyond. Human rights had become the unanswerable bottom line. In a multicultural environment with multiple religions and a good spread of secularism, human rights provided the one common point of reference for values. With the decline of a predominantly colonial Christian ideology, the danger of a relativist quagmire, in which social and governmental relations would be difficult to order, was real. In recent years the value system offered by human rights has increasingly filled the breach. Its universality has been sufficient to sustain a sophisticated apparatus of international law. And this, too, has had an impact on domestic law, not only because of requirements from international institutions, but also because of the infusion of an ethos and modus operandi. Thus in the UK the New Labour government was not only negotiating with international institutions and court rulings, but was also itself sufficiently imbued with a human rights commitment to voluntarily introduce the Human Rights Act; it introduced administrative arrangements to ensure human rights adherence and gave a boost to the role of the equality commissions, amalgamating them and establishing the Equality and Human Rights Commission (EHRC). The aim to reduce discrimination as part of the human rights project has had a large impact on family policy, particularly across gender and caring relations.

Towards the end of its administration New Labour even made the existential leap to adopt a social rights perspective. There had been pressure from Europe for it to do so for some time, with a growing tranche of case law from the European Court of Human Rights requiring family support services. The European Convention on Human Rights articles on freedom from inhuman and degrading treatment and respect for family life, as interpreted by the European Court of Human Rights, had been particularly influential in requiring local authorities to prevent child abuse and neglect where feasible, and in requiring them to commit resources to family services to facilitate the reunification of children in state care with their families (Henricson and Bainham, 2005). It was significant that provisions under the

European Convention on Human Rights were enforceable by those directly deprived of a right, thereby creating a relationship between citizen and international government that was capable of instigating change within national government institutions.

There was, too, a body of literature advocating a more creative social rights response. Henricson (2003, 2007) drew out the range of social rights that were implied in family services across financial support, health, education for children and young people, parenting support, information, advice and a range of therapeutic facilities. The request that these be specified as rights rather than fluid welfare provision was based on a perception that family support requirements exist nationwide and that, while they may vary according to the age and condition of the person, they have a universal core associated with health, wellbeing and the opportunity for fulfilment. They do not emanate from top-down prescription, but rather from the person with critical wants.

In their review of *The child and family policy divide*, Henricson and Bainham (2005) made the case for a social rights approach because of its capacity to inhibit distorted investment in favour of particular targets and particular interest groups and lobbies: 'They flush individual and collective entitlements out into the open. And they create a balance of interests that cannot disappear so readily as it might under a discretionary welfare model of government investment' (Henricson and Bainham, 2005, p 108). Rights were perceived as having the potential to provide a useful regulatory barometer and safety net in family services. They could also safeguard people who were unable to make themselves heard, either through the exertion of consumer choice, or through the ballot box because of their incapacity or disenfranchised or minority status: for example, incapacitated older people, young offenders, young people in care and families in child protection proceedings.

There had been disappointment in the early days of New Labour that the government had not engaged sufficiently with social rights and had been reluctant to move beyond basic civil rights regulation (Ruxton and Karim, 2001). While there were provisions for prospective legislation to be scanned for possible Human Rights Act contravention, it was considered that generally the opportunity for the Human Rights Act to inform the broad sweep of social policy had not been seized on as it might have been. The new EHRC had some potential, but the focus of its remit was equality of access rather than service expectation. It was suggested that the Human Rights Act could have been used more creatively to enhance the security and foundation of social welfare entitlements (Henricson, 2007).

For most of its period in office the New Labour government's approach was of a paternalistic, welfare-oriented persuasion. Latterly, however, there was an increasing interest in the role of bottom-up pressure to secure service improvement. David Miliband made a convincing case in *Empowerment and the deal for devolution*: 'Already 75% of local councils are experimenting with some form of citizen engagement. It needs to go further….There needs to be a new balance: more bottom up accountability, more horizontal accountability across public services through LSPs [Local Service Partnerships], and less top down accountability' (Miliband, 2006, pp 18-19).

A further lever was the imminent demise of the New Labour administration which motivated an attempt to hold onto the social supports created during its tenure by fixing them as rights. The strategy document *Building Britain's future* proposed a move: 'from a system based primarily on targets and central direction to one where individuals have enforceable entitlement over the service they receive' (Prime Minister, 2009, p 18).

## Social liberalism versus support and control

How did this social liberalism and human rights axis fit with the government's support and control agenda? Not altogether comfortably. While there were many features that were complementary, particularly in relation to reducing discrimination and supporting equality of opportunity, there were strains, significantly in relation to children's rights and the control of anti-social behaviour. There was, as we have seen, tension on the smacking front. To these strains must be added the difficulties that arose over Parenting Orders and ASBOs that confounded rights within the criminal justice system. The Commission on Families and the Wellbeing of Children summarised the disquiet that was widely articulated by commentators:

> ... the coercive nature of Parenting Orders have created, in effect, a questionable new reality of dual responsibility for juvenile crime....
>
> Criticisms of Antisocial Behaviour Orders are that they unduly infringe civil liberties, weaken due process, ignore existing criminal laws and "widen the net" of those subject to criminal sanctions. (Commission on Families and the Wellbeing of Children, 2005, pp 34/35)

Support was intertwined with this control and consequently implicated in the conflict with social liberalism. In this tension it is noteworthy that the support and control axis tended to prevail. It would not be unreasonable to surmise that the reason for this was that the drive for support and control, although it broadly chimed with the popular mood, was decidedly government-led.

## Support and control

The motives for the support and control elements of family policy under New Labour were multiple and accorded with common expectations of a range of government functions. These functions span matters of safety through to the reduction of poverty. In relation to family life they include the physical protection of children, social crime prevention and measures to promote effective childrearing that lessen the likelihood of delinquent development in children. They also entail the promotion of an economically productive and stable community. The provision of benefits and education, facilitating work and undertaking a variety of other measures to support the general viability of the family as an economic unit are pertinent here. These protective functions, and an adherence to a Christo-humanistic moral imperative in the tradition of Beveridge, drew New Labour to a philosophy concerned with the dual function of reducing social exclusion and creating a socially cohesive society. This went beyond the welfare state's baseline of providing a threshold of material wellbeing that families should not fall short of, to involve attention to relative deprivation, community integration and even moral regulation (Levitas, 1998; Henricson, 2003).

## Tensions in tackling social exclusion

Combating social exclusion and promoting social cohesion were very clearly articulated goals for the New Labour government's support and control agenda. However, its mode of addressing these matters had inner tensions. Targets for child poverty reduction were set, and, as we have seen, a range of redistributive tax and benefit measures were taken to deliver these. The measures had some beneficial effect, but inequality in the UK is deep and entrenched, and more was required. A major contraction of inequality was needed if child poverty was to be substantially reduced in accordance with the targets. Yet insufficient root and branch measures were taken to reduce inequality. Rather there was an acceptance of its rationale with the mushrooming of the financial sector exemplified in these often quoted words from Peter Mandelson: 'we [New Labour] are intensely relaxed about people getting filthy rich, so long as they pay their taxes'.

Cited by Mandelson at a Fabian conference when he was Business Secretary towards the end of New Labour's period in office, the logic for this distancing from any major redistribution exercise was reaffirmed. He advocated promoting equality of opportunity rather than 'seeking to impose equality of outcome through government policy'. He wished to tie liberal economics into a social democratic framework: 'There's a tendency, especially during a downturn, to make the incomes of the wealthy a proxy for fairness – that if we are reducing the incomes of the wealthy, that is somehow making us a fair society. And I think it is very important that we don't get ourselves into thinking that tax therefore, and tax on the highest paid in our society, is a litmus test of social justice...' (Mandelson, 2009). Mandelson contrasted 'the politics of resentment', which he deemed 'corrosive', with a politics based on aspiring to 'lift people up'. That, he considered, had been New Labour's record and achieved without raising the top rate of tax.

With this explicit, as well as implicit, acceptance of inequality, there was a focus instead on achieving social mobility and cohesion through personal development. Rather than engaging in significant programmes of redistribution, the drive was to facilitate enabling behaviours, and to this end family policy – family and parenting services in particular – lent itself as the appropriate tool. The political philosophy and mindset behind this was non-confrontational. Faced with a grossly unequal society, the response was not to tackle inequality head on, but rather to minimise equalities rhetoric and to seek to increase life chances through family services.

The pre-occupation with personal development through family provision can be seen not only from investment in programmes such as Sure Start and early years learning support initiatives, but also from the intense engagement with outcomes evidence. This was not a web of provision justified on the basis of support being offered as an act of collective kindness; evidence of delivering change was required, and in particular, change was sought in terms of social mobility. This was consequently an era of major evaluations following a similar model to that developed in the US. There was repeated reference to the evidence base in government policy documents. The findings of the study on the effective provision of pre-school education (Sylva et al, 2004), which demonstrated the effectiveness of good childcare and early learning facilities on child outcomes, were often cited by ministers and advisers. Parenting programmes were promoted that had evidence of effecting change, and these tended to be derived from the American–Australian axis, with their intensive evaluations, rather than home-grown systems that would have been rather more organic and less rigorously assessed (Henricson, 2007; Melhuish et al, 2007).

The scale of the initiatives and the preoccupation with understanding the impact and possibilities of changing behaviour are indicative of the New Labour government's commitment to a programme of family support and control in public policy able to deliver social mobility and cohesion. Early strategy documents also indicate that it was the government leading this process. The Commission for Social Justice, for example, made a substantial case for investment in families and children: 'Investment in their [children's] life chances is the best social and economic investment we can make' (Commission for Social Justice, 1994, p 320).

In *Supporting families*, one of the first strategies produced when New Labour took office, childcare and nursery education for the under-fives and strengthening parental responsibility were prioritised:

> 1.37 The early years of a child's life are critical to their future success and happiness. We are determined to invest in better opportunities for our youngest children and to support parents in preparing them to succeed at school and in life.
>
> 1.45 We need to do more to provide help to parents with the difficult job of raising children successfully throughout their childhood and adolescence. We want to improve the support for parents across the board. (Home Office, 1998, pp 15/16)

The New Labour government led the way with this family support and control programme and did so with the force of conviction. The programme was to some considerable degree underwritten by international and domestic influences external to government, but these influences facilitated rather than prompted the government's intent.

## European influence

There is no evidence that that this web of provision was instigated by EU directives. The EU's remit is primarily concerned with issues associated with work and migrant labour – hence its rather extensive influence in the work–life balance field as we have seen. Other aspects of family policy, however, fall outside its direct remit and legal competence. There has, nevertheless, been some encouragement to member states to develop family policies. The EU Parliament recommended the institution of a 'comprehensive family policy', which would encourage member states to address the needs of families in new legislation and harmonise policies relating to families across Europe as appropriate (Resolution on Family Policy in the EC [1983] OJ C184/116). A further resolution exhorted member states to: 'conduct specific family policies supporting and protecting the family financially and its role as an educational force' and 'to take account in their policy of the needs and requirements of families' (Resolution on the Protection of Families and Children [1999] OJ C128/79, No 3). However, these declarations were not binding and therefore of limited impact, causing McGlynn (2001) to summarise the situation somewhat negatively, finding that the EU's regulation of family policy to have been undertaken in a fragmented manner as a corollary to other policy strands.

In terms of the legal situation there is more potential for influence through the European Convention on Human Rights and the Council of Europe. As we have seen, the clauses in the Convention asserting the right to respect for family life and freedom from inhuman and degrading treatment had some impact in terms of encouraging family support from a social rights perspective.

Notwithstanding the growing role of European institutions in family policy, the evidence suggests that there have been limitations in terms of their influence on strategic development. Overall they constituted a contributory but not dominant factor in influencing New Labour's programme of shaping family life through support and control – an endeavour with which it, as the national government, was wholly engaged.

## Public attitudes

In terms of public attitudes, New Labour was not going against the grain of the country's mood with its support and control measures. It was not imposing on an unwilling population. Rather, its agenda worked well with an increasingly inclusive society that had emerged as a result of growing prosperity and communications technology; British society was no longer complicit in ghettos where different standards applied to which the establishment turned a blind eye. Instead there were expectations of norms of behaviour, education and living conditions – a homogenisation of social standards.

There was also a reaction against the social fragmentation that had held sway during the 1980s when Margaret Thatcher notoriously announced that: 'There is no such thing as society' (Thatcher, 1987). The role of the state in supporting families and children was ripe for re-negotiation in the direction of enhancement (Henricson et al, 2001). Further underpinning this were pervasive anxieties that parenting needed help in the face of the deterioration of community networks and associated higher levels of criminality and anti-social behaviour. Advocates of communitarianism such as Etzioni spoke of a 'parenting deficit' that needed to be rectified (Etzioni, 1993), and the link between parenting and crime was increasingly vocalised in public debate (Utting et al, 1993).

There was also evidence of endorsement – indeed encouragement of New Labour's interventionist approach from the caring professions and policy influencers that make up swathes of the statutory sector and civil society. A survey of these groups on the future of family services produced the following schedule of universal and specialist services that was both ambitious and fitting in the context of the government's caring vision.

> Telephone support; Facilitated parenting group/
> course; Self-help parenting group; Intergenerational
> learning; Parent/child recreation activities; Drop in
> centres; Mentoring/volunteering help in the home;
> Other respite support; Individual counselling/support
> in the home or clinic; Social services child protection;
> Relationship support/couple counselling. Taken as a
> whole, the body of services should include support
> for mothers and fathers in respect of children of all
> ages. Issues, such as disabilities and mental health
> and behavioural problems should be addressed, and
> significant cultural groups should be catered for.
> Open access should be offered where possible, to
> be facilitated through extensive publicity targeting,
> in particular, hard to reach parents eg fathers, black
> parents. (Henricson, 2002, p 6)

Surveys of the wider population also showed that, while family and friends were still the mainstay of family support, other professional and volunteer-based facilities were welcome. A MORI survey found that 69 per cent of adults believed that support, training or counselling could make a difference to resolving problems in families, but that almost a third of parents did not know where to go for help (National Family and Parenting Institute, 1999). Ghate and Hazel (2001) found that, although they did not want provision to be intrusive, parents wished to receive family services. As parenting television programmes such as *Supernanny* came onto the scene, their popularity demonstrated the appetite among parents for some level of help. A survey conducted in 2006 revealed that almost three quarters of parents had watched at least one programme, with more than 80 per cent of those watching considering it to have been useful (Ipsos MORI, 2006). Research into more formal family support programmes found that they, too, were valued by parents and had benefits for most users (Buchanan, 1999; Statham, 2000). Evaluations of parenting programmes showed a common theme of regret among participants that support had not been provided sooner, albeit that drop-out rates were often high (Ghate and Ramella, 2002). The demand for support with children's special needs constantly outstripped enhanced provision, as did requests for counselling and adolescent and mental health services (Commission on Families and the Wellbeing of Children, 2005). Possibly most convincing has been the popularity of children's centres established nationwide, with high levels of use and a resulting commitment not to dismantle them by the Conservative opposition in the election of 2010 (Apps et al, 2007; Conservative Party, 2010).

Nevertheless there were some tensions with perceptions of excessive state involvement. In terms of the justice system, civil liberties and children's rights, we have seen the anxieties expressed by legal and social welfare commentators. Parenting Orders were challenged despite the support provided under their auspices being welcomed once parents engaged with programmes (Ghate and Ramella, 2002; Commission on Families and the Wellbeing of Children, 2005). There was a broad spectrum of doubters across those engaged in delivering youth justice (Henricson, 2003).

Civil libertarian issues aside, there was a literature critical of a support enterprise that presupposed certain standards of behaviour – norms that were deemed middle class (Klett-Davies, 2010). Countering this was a substantial cohort of family service providers – psychiatrists, social workers, parenting practitioners, home support volunteers and more – who instead accepted and advocated the common requirements of 'authoritative parenting' (Baumrind, 1967; Commission on Families and the Wellbeing of Children, 2005).

Nevertheless the challenges went beyond a few class-conscious academics. The caring state was deemed to be overbearing in some instances among the wider population. Rejection of attempts to improve the diets of children with nutritious school dinners was an example. Health and safety measures were habitually ridiculed in the media. Parents were deemed to be the subject of constant nagging and even of being deskilled by the constant dictate about how things should be done. Parents' anxieties over losing autonomy emerged in a number of surveys of their perceptions of their support requirements (Ghate and Hazel, 2001; Cragg et al, 2002) sufficient to draw the following comment: 'The question that needs to be borne in mind, however, is whether parents' authority in relation to their children is being maintained sufficiently intact to encourage them, the parents, to shoulder willingly the caring responsibilities that are expected of them' (Henricson and Bainham, 2005).

The New Labour government was at one level aware of the dangers of excessive intervention, as Jack Straw indicated in his preface to *Supporting families*:

> ... governments have to be wary about intervening in areas of private life and intimate emotion. We in government need to approach family policy with a strong dose of humility. We must not preach and we must not give the impression that members of the government are any better than the rest of the population in meeting the challenge of family life. They are not. (Home Office, 1998, p 4)

There was recognition that governments should not dictate family formation, but control through kindness was not a fault that was recognised. Certainly little heed appeared to be taken of the ambivalent sentiments that were evident in the popular response, and the Coalition government was able to tap into a strata of resentment towards the trait in New Labour that was often termed 'nannying'. There was a backlash of moderate proportions that the new government was able to utilise as it combined the promotion of liberal social freedom with a cost-cutting agenda.

## Overview

In this chapter we have glimpsed the multiplicity of roots that contributed to family policy during the New Labour period in office. There was a symbiotic relationship between the different strands, with several, and often all, applying to each aspect of family policy. We have seen the role of public attitudes across socially liberal measures and the support and control functions of government. There have been international influences relating to both ethos and governance, and closely associated with human rights. There has been the not insignificant force of civil society – vociferous thinkers and campaigners in the field. And finally there has been the internal dynamic and preoccupations of the New Labour government itself. Where there has been a difference it has related to degree of influence, with the principal divergence being between socially liberal measures on the one hand, and support and control on the other.

The latter, support and control, was distinctive in having New Labour's core governmental theme and *raison d'être* as the lead driver. That theme and credo might be summarised as a commitment to promote social inclusion and cohesion through a programme of parenting and child behaviour change among families who had been excluded or who had failed to achieve, with some tax and benefits support, but without directly confronting the entrenched and substantial inequalities of income that typify British society. It was not a motive prompting the development of an integrated family policy across the generations; rather it led to a focus on the young. In Chapter Five we consider what was wrong with this approach, notwithstanding the many positive aspects of New Labour's family policy that we have witnessed.

# FOUR

# The legacy and the Coalition government

On assuming office in 2010 the Conservative/Liberal Coalition government did not have a fully prepared detailed family programme based on a coherent philosophy. In contrast, in 1997, with years of preparation behind it, New Labour had been ready to take action implementing its particular socially ambitious communitarian brand of family policy. While the Conservative Party in opposition had indeed formulated proposals with the support of Iain Duncan Smith's Centre for Social Justice, the government taking the reins in 2011 was in a very different position from its predecessor on various fronts. Harold Macmillan's warning to "beware events dear boy, beware events" was highly pertinent. The Coalition government was faced with a series of extraneous factors, some of which constrained its room for manoeuvre, while others may have facilitated measures that a number of its members wished to take in relation to family policy. For those whose intent was to roll back the frontiers of the state, reducing aspects of family services would have been difficult to embark on without the imperative of the economic crisis.

The 'events' in question broadly fall into three categories:

- the international economic crash having implications for cuts in government spending;
- the election resulting in the formulation of a coalition government that has had to accommodate different strands of political conviction;
- the very dimensions and characteristics of the family policy implemented under New Labour over 13 years having in many ways become entrenched and the norm, forcing a

relationship of response rather than initiation on its successor government.

These three influences operating in an intertwining fashion have shaped the current government's actions and direction of policy to a substantial degree.

## Social liberalism

In the wake of New Labour's social liberalism, which way has the Coalition government turned? Has it been socially liberal or socially conservative? The evidence to date suggests that neither of these labels fully describes the Coalition's activities. Rather a midway position has been adopted with a melee of explanatory drivers.

### Human rights and family forms

The Conservative Party has had many reservations about the 1998 Human Rights Act, and indeed nurtured proposals to replace it with a less forthright instrument, a UK Bill of Rights (Conservative Party, 2010). The reservations voiced related very much to external intrusion into government and a range of legal actions across the public estate. In the event, the downsizing of the Human Rights Act is unlikely to take place while there is a Liberal Democrat wing in government.

The Conservative strand of the Coalition has itself shown no intention to clip or reverse New Labour's socially liberal enactments associated with recognising different family forms and non-discrimination relating to gender and sexual orientation. The 2004 Civil Partnership Act is accepted and even supported, with further proposals for marriage to be made available to gay couples, and there is no evidence that the 2006 and 2010 Equality Acts will be reversed. This concurrence with advances made in relation to social liberalism is partly indicative of a change in social attitudes nationally, as described in Chapter Three. It is also a repetition of a familiar pattern in the development and acceptance of socially liberal measures. Such measures tend to be brought in by Labour administrations, as with the anti-discrimination and equality laws introduced in the 1960s and 1970s under Premiers Wilson and Callaghan, and then to continue under, although not initiated by, successor Conservative governments.

The issue of the reinstatement of preferential tax treatment for married couples is a significant exception here. Trailed in the Conservative manifesto with considerable publicity and associated controversy, the proposal to reinstate the married couple's allowance was not dropped as a concession to the Liberal Democrats in Coalition negotiations, although the Liberal Democrats did maintain the right to abstain in parliamentary voting on the subject (Conservative Party, 2010; HM Government, 2010b).

## Work and care

In the work–care domain, the array of legislation on work–life balance and employment has become so integrated into the country's social fabric that the bulk may be expected to remain intact. However, while under New Labour there was active promotion of socially liberal equality between the sexes, under the Coalition government there has been some ambivalence. We have seen an extension of leave for fathers under a scheme proposed by the former government (Clegg, 2011). However, in contrast to this work–care facility, there has been a curtailment of access to childcare through a reduction of the childcare element of the Working Tax Credit. The new requirement will be for the state to pay a maximum of 70 per cent of childcare costs, rather than the current 80 per cent, from 2011/12 (HM Treasury, 2010). This may be construed as indicative of a return to the previous Conservative government's view in the 1980s and 1990s that the resourcing of childcare is a private affair (Pascall, 2006). Certainly it has prompted concerns to be voiced by the national childcare organisation, the Daycare Trust.

The cut equates to a loss of up to £1,560 per year for families who are already struggling with the burden of extortionate childcare costs.... Parents in the UK contribute more towards childcare costs than any other OECD country, and this will be made more difficult after these announcements, even after taking account of the increase in the Child Tax Credit. Furthermore, this is on top of cuts already announced in the June budget such as the abolition of the Child Trust Fund, the restriction of eligibility for the Sure Start Maternity Grant to the first child and the abolition of the Health in Pregnancy Grant. (Daycare Trust, 2010, p 3)

It is noteworthy that this childcare cut also coincides with a significant decline in the availability of female employment (TUC, 2010). New Labour's aim to reduce poverty through supporting female employment – and indeed the promotion of gender equality generally – appears to be less of an imperative for this government. There is instead a rather more substantial focus on deficit reduction in the nation's finances, which we shall see has prompted cost-cutting measures across family support.

## Support and control

Support clearly has substantial resource implications for governments. Arguably under the Coalition, support has been in receipt of a great deal more attention, change and retrenchment than most of New Labour's socially liberal measures for the simple reason that it costs. It is also closely associated with the left–right political divide concerning attitudes towards markets and redistribution.

### Financial support

In terms of financial support, there are likely to be serious implications for child poverty from the deficit reduction programme. The Institute for Fiscal Studies found in their analysis of the Treasury's 2010 Spending Review that families with children would suffer most from the proposed cuts, and that they were regressive: 'The Treasury's modelling shows that the benefit measures announced yesterday will hit those at the bottom half of the income distribution more as a share of their income than those in the top half' (Emmerson, 2010, p 2).

The Institute for Fiscal Studies has estimated that the Coalition government's reforms will increase relative poverty by 100,000 children in 2012-13, and that they will increase absolute poverty by 200,000 children. The estimate for 2013-14 is worse, with Coalition reforms acting to increase absolute poverty by some 300,000 children (Brewer and Joyce, 2010). These figures contrast with the fall in child poverty in 2009-10 when, according to Office for National Statistics, child poverty decreased to 20 per cent, down from 22 per cent the previous year (Elliot and Wintour, 2011).

Measures taken by the Coalition government that are likely to have a detrimental impact include:

- the freezing and reduction of a range of tax credits and entitlements, including child benefit;
- caps and reductions relating to local housing allowance rates which will mean that many, in particular larger, families will no longer be able to continue to live in their homes;
- a reduction of 10 per cent in Council Tax Benefit, with decisions about who gets support localised introducing uncertainty and a lack of transparency in benefit decisions;
- the use of the Consumer Price Index as the basis for up-rating benefits and tax credits, reducing their value in real terms by 1.5 per cent;
- the abolition of the Health in Pregnancy Grant and the baby element of the Child Tax Credit, and the restriction of the Sure Start Maternity Grant to the first child;
- the abolition of the Child Trust Fund.

There has been an increase in Child Tax Credit and a rise in the threshold for taxation. While these measures are helpful for poorer families, they will not compensate for the cuts specified above and a rise in Value Added Tax that is affecting basic household goods (Emmerson, 2010; Family and Parenting Institute, 2010).

The 2010 Child Poverty Act remains on the statute book, but there are currently no fiscal measures being taken to further its aim of reducing child poverty; rather the reverse. An argument has been put forward by the Coalition that there has been a misplaced emphasis on income redistribution and benefits to address the problem of poverty; the intention now is to re-focus on issues associated with wellbeing and opportunities for fulfilment (DWP and DfE, 2011). There is thus some alignment with New Labour's concern to develop personal potential and thereby to enhance child outcomes. What is missing, however, is the other side of the equation, the balance of financial support that was provided under the previous government.

The whole approach is encapsulated in the Coalition's first national child poverty strategy, *A new approach to child poverty*, which makes the following statement of direction: 'At its heart are strengthening families, encouraging responsibility, promoting work, guaranteeing of fairness and providing support for the most vulnerable' (DWP and DfE, 2011).

## Personal development and family services

The Coalition has made considerable progress in planning its personal development policy directions. Following New Labour's initiative on happiness and wellbeing, it has embarked on the development of a national measurement facility. The Office for National Statistics has been commissioned to establish wellbeing indicators through a consultation exercise (ONS, 2011a), and the first measure of the nation's wellbeing has been conducted.

The early years of childhood – pre-birth to five years of age – has been another major focal point with a series of widely publicised reports produced. Frank Field and Graham Allen, both Labour Members of Parliament, have written 'independent' reports for the Coalition, taking forward the personal development theme as a response to poverty. Graham Allen (2011) addressed the scope of early intervention programmes, placing an emphasis on changing parenting behaviour. Access to Family Nurse Partnerships for first-time mothers, a national parenting campaign and access to quality pre-school education are all proposed. There are also recommendations for the generation of income from non-governmental sources, with a process of returns on investment related to long-term savings as a result of enhanced children's outcomes.

Frank Field's strategic document was conceived as an anti-poverty report, but its remit was clearly steered away from addressing current financial inequalities to focus on the non-fiscal elements of wellbeing.

The aim of the review is to:

- Generate a broader debate about the nature and extent of poverty in the UK;
- Examine the case for reforms to poverty measures, in particular for the inclusion of non-financial elements;
- Explore how a child's home environment affects their chances of being ready to take full advantage of their schooling; and
- Recommend potential action by government and other institutions to reduce poverty and enhance life chances for the least advantaged, consistent with the Government's fiscal strategy. (Field, 2010, p 5)

Certainly the thrust of the report's recommendations are removed from the realm of tax credits and benefits, and entirely geared towards personal development and early years upbringing. As well as 'life chances indicators', it proposes the establishment of a 'foundation years' policy stream covering the period from the womb to five years of age. There is even a recommendation that could increase child poverty by diverting inflation protection rises in financial support for disadvantaged families to early years service provision. In the event, in his 2011 Autumn statement the Chancellor of the Exchequer brought in an extension of free early learning nursery facilities to 40 per cent of two-year-olds, while Child Tax Credits were reduced and the couple and lone-parent element of the Working Tax Credit frozen (Osborne, 2011).

A further report in this area has been Tickell's (2011) review of the early years foundation stage that was established by New Labour in 2008. A series of recommendations are made for working more closely with parents, as well as simplifying the goals and assessments of early years, and improving the training of the workforce.

Many of the proposals in these reports were brought together in a policy statement on provision for the early years, *Families in the foundation years* (DfE, 2011a). They were also summarised in the report *Opening doors, breaking barriers: A strategy for social mobility* (Cabinet Office, 2011). Broadly the interest in the foundation years is linked to the Coalition's interest in social mobility as a theme.

> We both want a Britain where social mobility is unlocked; where everyone, regardless of background has the chance to rise as high as their talents and ambitions allow them. (HM Government, 2010b, p 7)

> Income at any one point in time is, of course, important. But it doesn't tell you everything about a person's life chances, or the life chances of their children, about the ability people have to get ahead. And you simply cannot overestimate the role that parents play in that. (Clegg, 2011)

This series of policy documents do not demonstrate a new approach. Rather they continue the thrust of New Labour's emphasis on investing in services to support the upbringing of children, particularly in the early stages of life. Sure Start was a prime example of New Labour's initiatives in this area, as was the infrastructure concerned with delivering parenting programmes and supporting early home learning. Differences coming from the Coalition have largely been around a decline in the service investment available and a reduction in direct financial support to families.

The practical reality on the ground has seen family services contract. The Early Intervention Grant to local authorities is 11 per cent less than the funding streams it amalgamates (BBC, 2010), and the dwindling of local government resources has already had its impact with Sure Start closures underway. The popularity of Sure Start children's centres secured a commitment to their preservation prior to the election (Conservative Party, 2010). However, the withdrawal of the ring fence that ensured their funding has made them vulnerable to cuts by councils that are strapped for cash (HM Treasury, 2010). A survey of Sure Start children's centres found that 250 were at risk of closing within a year, with a further 2,000 cutting back on the services they offer to families and 1,000 issuing 'risk of redundancy notices' to staff (4children and Daycare Trust, 2011). Other impacts, for example, on voluntary sector provision, parenting programmes, special needs support and social care may be anticipated. Indeed cuts across the whole support fabric are being reported, although they are yet to be fully audited.

One of the themes to emerge both in the discourse within the Conservative Party prior to the election and in subsequent directions has been a move away from population-wide facilities to targeted provision. While there is a commitment to promote health visiting, the reduction of universal services is the general approach. For example, Sure Start children's centres are to redirect their services towards children most in need: 'We will take Sure Start back to its original purpose of early intervention, increase its focus on the neediest families...' (HM Government, 2010b, p 19).

Cost-cutting and targeting is then the dominant theme, and it may be construed that the vision for major social change that informed New Labour's activities is no longer a pivotal rationale. Rather the approach is one of responding to services that have already been established, and limiting these. Family support has been cut substantially, rather more in respect of financial help to families on low incomes than in relation to services or support in kind. But services too are experiencing significant contraction as a result of a reduction in the flow of resources from central to local government. The frontiers of the state grew substantially under New Labour in relation to family support, and undoubtedly there is a will, certainly among the Conservative partners in the Coalition government, to roll back those frontiers. The cost-cutting rationale in tightened economic circumstances has to some degree enabled this.

New Labour's vision of social change is likely to be further compromised by the emphasis placed by the Coalition on localism and the 'Big Society', with its diverse public, private and voluntary delivery mechanisms for public services. The White Paper *Open public services* (HM Government, 2011) describes this policy theme. While increasing the local direction of public services, both concepts reduce the degree to which central government can pursue social goods through shaping the social welfare landscape.

There was a branch of localism advocated by New Labour as latterly it pulled back from a target culture and sought to give more creative space to local and professional initiative (Miliband, 2006). There was, however, an expectation that the bulk of services would be constant. The strategies in *Every child matters* (HM Treasury, 2003) and *Every parent matters* (DfES, 2007) were all in place and would remain. The crusade against child poverty would not be undercut. Localism was instead something of a post hoc add-on. In a cost-cutting scenario the opposite is true. With a large proportion of the Coalition's cuts having been apportioned to central government's grant to local authorities – a 28 per cent cut (HM Treasury, 2010) – local discretion is largely concerned with where the axe should fall. While duties concerned with baseline child protection and other core social care functions in family services may be expected to direct priorities, there are concerns over what might not be delivered. There is a case for enhancing central direction at a time of economic stringency, in the interests of postcode fairness and ensuring that critical needs are met.

Arguably the Big Society may also detract from cohesive service provision. With a variety of undefined providers, fluid responsibilities and a contracting voluntary sector in the wake of local authorities' cuts, there may be greater insecurity for those who are reliant on social supports.

## Child protection and cutting bureaucracy

On the child protection front the Coalition has sought to reduce controls on professionals in another move away from centralised government. A report was commissioned by the Department for Education from Professor Eileen Munro addressing issues of concern relating to levels of procedural bureaucracy and a diminution of professional discretion:

> I set out recommendations that I believe will, taken together, help to reform the child protection system from being over-bureaucratised and concerned with compliance to one that keeps a focus on children, checking whether they are being effectively helped, and adapting when problems are identified.
>
> A move away from compliance to a learning culture will require those working in child protection to be given more scope to exercise professional judgement in deciding how best to help children and their families. (Munro, 2011, p 5)

Away from the cost-cutting scene, there is no reason to suppose that this encouragement of professional discretion will detract from services. Rather there is a convincing argument that the shoring up of procedures in the wake of anxieties over mismanaged child abuse cases may have hampered the social worker–client relationship (Cooper et al, 2003). The Coalition has also closed ContactPoint, the national child database, because of perceived civil liberty issues. ContactPoint was originally set up by New Labour to enhance agency liaison on child protection matters. The jury is still out as to whether this closure will have negative implications for cohesive interagency working.

## Criminal justice

The action taken by the Coalition on child protection has a distinctly liberal flavour. Interestingly, however, this has not extended to controls within the criminal justice system. The civil liberty reservations voiced in some quarters over Parenting Orders and ASBOs have not resulted in the introduction of a light touch alternative system. While ASBOs are set to disappear, an array of new orders is proposed in a Coalition consultation on the subject. They include a Community Trigger to force agency action, a Criminal Behaviour Order controlling behaviour after conviction, Crime Prevention Injunctions, breach of which could result in imprisonment, Community Protection Orders involving place-specific powers for local authorities and the police, and police 'direction' powers enabling the police to direct individuals who are likely to cause a crime or disorder away from a particular place (Home Office, 2011). In terms of compromising civil liberties these provisions appear to match ASBOs. Furthermore, to date, there is no evidence that Parenting Orders are to be dropped or significantly changed.

Following the August 2011 riots, when the spark of a police demonstration escalated into gang aggression and opportunistic criminal activity, a law and order stance has been more heavily profiled. Proposals have ranged from area curfews (May, 2011) to evicting perpetrators' families from social housing and a recasting of the operation of the European Convention on Human Rights, with the Human Rights Act blamed for a diminution of personal responsibility in society. Heavier approaches to the punishment of criminal behaviour have also been encouraged (Cameron, 2011). The riots have seen a reaffirmation of governmental commitment to the family with a continuation of New Labour's intensive work with troubled families. A 'family test' is to be introduced for government activity to encourage adult couple rather than single parenting to redress what is perceived as moral and behavioural decline (Cameron, 2011).

## Adult care

As with family services associated with the upbringing of children, the Coalition's response to the needs of the elderly population appears somewhat ambivalent. While there are some steps being taken that are supportive, these are being undermined because of the context of substantial cuts to resources.

In terms of financial support there has been an apparent commitment to sustain the living standards of the older generation. In its analysis of the 2010 Spending Review, the Institute for Fiscal Studies found that: 'The cuts to welfare spending mean that benefits will be focussed more on pensioners and less on families with children...' (Emmerson, 2010). However, this policy direction has been counterbalanced by a bringing forward of the rise in the age people are expected to work to prior to receiving a state pension. There have been complaints over the lack of time prospective pensioners, in particular women, have had to prepare for the changes. The 2011 Pensions Bill provides that the state pension age for women will rise from 60 to 65 years by 2018, which Age UK considers to be insufficient notice for people on tight budgets to be able to make the necessary financial adjustment (Age UK, 2011b).

As with other family services, social care for older people will be subject to the range of public service reforms proposed in the *Open public services* White Paper (HM Government, 2011), with the associated uncertainties. It will also, significantly, be subject to local authority spending cuts. The predicament facing governments of all persuasions as to how to realistically fund and sustain standards in social care continues to form a critical area of debate. Where should the line be drawn between personal and state responsibility?

A number of reports have been produced taking forward the early explorations by New Labour of the future of elder care. *A vision for adult social care: Capable communities and active citizens* (DH, 2010) sets out the Coalition's perspective. It promotes greater user involvement in service delivery and the establishment of a Big Society diverse provider market. There is some recognition that standards in care might be jeopardised by this approach, and safeguarding arrangements are proposed to address the risk. The Law Commission has produced a report to Parliament on *Adult social care* (2011) that places a premium on consistency. It recommends that basic national standards of support be specified and for local authorities to be required to establish Safeguarding Adults Boards. In terms of finance, the Commission on Funding of Care and Support (2011) in its report has recommended greater definition and standardisation of the financial contribution required of service users. There are proposals that the means-tested threshold be extended, that a cap be placed on personal contributions and that national eligibility criteria be established.

There has been a welcome move in these reports on adult services to increase levels of consistency and fairness. However, there are tensions because of the context of local authority spending cuts and the advocacy of Big Society diverse delivery mechanisms that may undermine a consistent approach. The direction of implementation has yet to be established, and a clearer picture may emerge with the issuing of a proposed White Paper and Social Care Reform Bill.

Significantly for the future of family policy, like New Labour, the Coalition has failed to break the mould of the separation that exists between children and adults' policies. There is no intergenerational assessment leading to a fair distribution of resources across the generations, and a whole family approach is not apparent either at a population level, or in relation to services provided to individual families. While fairness is an often cited aspiration, there is no coherent analysis or vision as to what might constitute 'fair' resource distribution across the generations.

## Overview

In summary, the Coalition's stance has been to respond to the legacy it inherited rather than to enter the family policy arena with a strategic programme. Some themes emerge from activities to date, but an all-encompassing philosophy informing the direction of policy is not apparent.

There has been relatively little change in relation to the socially liberal measures introduced by the last government, specifically in the area of family formation, and currently systems of rights regulation remain intact. The stance reflects both a lack of inclination for change and possibly a dose of liberalism.

The controversial controls in the criminal justice system, in particular those relating to anti-social behaviour and parental responsibility, also remain intact, albeit renamed. They are distinctly non-liberal. Child protection, too, remains largely as it was, although the move towards some relaxation of the procedural requirements that have developed has been noted, and the dropping of national data base monitoring is a step towards a loosening of government controls.

The story is substantially different across financial and service supports. Here we have seen a combination of the imperatives of cuts and an underlying conviction that the state's intervention has been over-extended. A premium has been placed on greater self-reliance.

Given that the spectrum of support for families will be substantially depleted and that overall family policy lacks a clear narrative, there will be a need for a future progressive government to re-grasp the issue, and in the light of recent experience, to develop a framework that is both principled and realistic in the interests of sustaining family wellbeing.

# FIVE

# What was wrong?

We have seen the scale and character of the New Labour family policy legacy. The difference and strength of the dynamic across the social liberalism and support and control fronts has been tracked and found to be both substantial and profound, with its roots in a narrative that sees family policy as a major player in the drive towards the 'good society', one which is more inclusive, cohesive and fair.

While the Coalition government has not engaged with the magnitude of the aspiration, no alternative has been conceptualised and promulgated. Rather there has been acquiescence in the measures taken, albeit with curtailment of investment by an administration defined by spending cuts. Some drive to change behaviours and child outcomes associated with the upbringing of children is still in evidence, with the main upfront state contraction being concerned with financial support rather than an in principle decision to detract from family services.

Should a future progressive government, then, simply continue from where New Labour left off? Should its purpose be one of returning to that momentum with little or no change of direction? Or is there a critique of New Labour's record and overall approach that needs to be taken on board in a debate on the options for family policy as it goes into another phase of development?

There are few who would cavil with some of the broad social goods that were achieved over the last 13 years – in particular those goods which enhanced family wellbeing. Unfortunately we do not have a regular national indicator set or measure of family wellbeing. But we do have some gauges of public opinion, as noted in Chapter Three, which, coupled with a degree of common-sense interpretation, enables a partial assessment to be made as to what may be interpreted as positive government achievements. Such an assessment is inevitably influenced by values, and from a progressive perspective the values set out in Chapter One provide direction.

The socially liberal measures introduced may not have appealed to relatively minor elements of social conservatism in British society, but by and large, as we have seen from attitudinal studies, they have been in accordance with trends of public opinion and have been assimilated. Socially liberal measures have reinforced a tolerant trend in family relations, bringing formerly marginalised relationships into the mainstream of family life and social acceptance. Since the Civil Partnership Act came into force in 2005 some 46,620 civil partnerships have taken place (ONS, 2011b). Children of single/lone parents have acquired the same financial support as children of married parents. In terms of the work–care divide, the measures taken in terms of child-associated leave, work flexibility and childcare services have all eased the dual burden of earning and caring, as well as introducing greater equality in gender relations. While there are concerns over male take-up of paternity leave associated with residual male earner social attitudes and pressures in the workplace (James, 2009), the choices available supporting flexible and more equal gender relations have undoubtedly increased.

On the support front, there are few who would wish to detract from the help that families have received under the auspices of New Labour, except perhaps those committed in principle to rolling back the state. Some may say that there was extravagance when assessing what the state could afford to pay, but helping families bring up children through financial and service supports is a broadly accepted social obligation.

Child poverty was substantially reduced over a relatively short time span, bearing in mind the time generally needed to effect shifts in income distribution. Elder poverty was also significantly reduced over New Labour's period in office. It is noteworthy that the former was a considerable feat that no other country has managed to achieve over a similar time span (OECD, 2008b; Miliband, 2010).

In relation to support services, the popularity and take-up of provision in children's centres suggests that families have found the facilities helpful and a resource that most would wish to see continue (Apps et al, 2007). Prior to 1997 there had been a significant gap in support for parents between the conclusion of early post-birth visits from health visitors and starting nursery school at age four (Henricson et al, 2001). That critical support during some of the most formative years of a child's life and a period of vulnerability for parents, particularly for those who may experience isolation, is now largely in place; we have a network of children's centres, childcare and early learning facilities.

These various achievements constitute a creditable record by any reckoning. Why, then, is there a residual sense of dissatisfaction that goes beyond anxiety that the structure may fall apart in the wake of the current government's austerity measures? There is a need to address this dissatisfaction and to understand the common and less familiar perceptions of the shortcomings of family policy under New Labour. An assessment of the scope, nature and legitimacy of the complaints is required in order to have a clear view of the possibilities for the future.

So as to make that assessment, this chapter looks at four specific but related issues:

- the question of targets and the impact they have had on raising false expectations and skewing services;
- the possibility that there have been inflated expectations of securing population behaviour change in relation to parenting, criminal behaviour and work–care gender relations;
- the inappropriateness of the expectation that changes in the family environment brought about by government policy could produce a substantial shift in the direction of poverty reduction and greater equality in economic relations;
- the failure to redress the fragmentary nature of family policy and to consider government resource allocation in the context of the whole family across the generations, continuing instead the tendency to respond to the needs of specific groups in relative isolation.

## Perceptions and those targets

The point might fairly be made that, if ever a government set itself up to fail, it was the New Labour government operating in hock to the management tool of targets. Targets were applied to all aspects of its endeavour, and they were honestly deployed; there is no evidence of their being set deliberately low in order to ensure delivery, thereby guaranteeing favourable news headlines. Rather the reverse was the case. It would not be unreasonable to conclude that the targets set were over-ambitious, with the almost inevitable consequence of securing pessimistic reporting on social enhancements that might in ordinary circumstances have been viewed as major achievements.

Targets were deployed in various forms, ranging from broad national aspirations to specific programme evaluations. They were used as an everyday tool as the public sector became increasingly geared towards a model of management by objectives. Some target setting in particular hit the headlines and will have had an impact on the public's perception of how the government was doing. Two prime examples in the family arena are the national child poverty targets and the evaluation of the flagship Sure Start programme. The missing of targets in both these cases may have contributed to a common perception of failed endeavour.

### Child poverty

As we have seen, child poverty was significantly reduced under New Labour. While this was recognised, it tended to be done so grudgingly in some progressive quarters. In their assessment of the record, Polly Toynbee and David Walker (2010) reflected: 'Labour stopped inequality from getting worse. Child poverty would have been 6 to 9% higher without their measures. The Gini coefficient of inequality would have gone up three points rather than the two it did under New Labour' (Toynbee and Walker, 2010).

Commentaries in reports from research organisations and charities at the forefront of the campaign to reduce poverty were habitually prone to reflect on the government's targets. Thus, for example, in the following assessment of the government's progress from the Joseph Rowntree Foundation, while there was an acknowledgement of the advances and the effectiveness of the tax and benefits system introduced, the focus of attention was on how the targets could be met, with a pessimistic pronouncement that the measures needed would be unlikely to be taken:

- Since the late 1990s, child poverty has started to fall, helped by rising parental employment and by large increases in tax credits and benefits paid to low income families with children.
- The Government could meet its target of halving child poverty between 1998 and 2010 by spending an estimated £4 billion a year (0.3 per cent of GDP) more than currently planned on tax and benefits.
.... The results show that the net effect of such (New Labour) policies will be to keep child poverty roughly at its present level by 2010 and reduce it by only 260, 000 by 2020. Far from 'ending' child poverty, this would only be enough to reach the missed 2004 target. (Hirsch, 2006, pp 1-4)

The focus of the debate was inevitably drawn towards the government's self-imposed targets, and with these now enshrined in legislation, it may be presumed that this will continue. With such a hostage to fortune at stake, the question must arise as to how these targets were arrived at. For example, was there some form of feasibility assessment? On the face of it, it seems not, or if there was, it must have been significantly flawed, bearing in mind the trends in escalating incomes at the top of the range which would inevitably have depressed incomes at the bottom in relative terms; Frank Field (2010) has commented that reaching the child poverty targets is simply impossible.

The reality is that people were pleasantly surprised and even astounded when Tony Blair made his resounding pledge to halve child poverty by 2010 and to end it by 2020 (Field, 2010). These were ballpark figures borne more of conviction than likelihood. The targets may have stretched the will of government, but they also left something of a feeling of despondency despite the creditable advances made.

There was, too, an element of the government engaging closely with poverty activists. Rather than repudiating criticisms, New Labour worked closely together with organisations such as the Joseph Rowntree Foundation, End Child Poverty Now and other campaigning organisations. This was not an exercise in masochism; rather there were ties of sympathy between a left of centre government and progressive lobby groups. There was also a view that the vocalisation of poverty concerns by such groups might shift public opinion in favour of government investment in redistribution, and certainly there was an uphill struggle on that score, with attitudinal studies suggesting that poverty is not viewed by the UK population as being a problem (see, for example, Castell and Thompson, 2007). While this motivation might be considered laudable, it may have rebounded to some degree in giving the narrative of a failure to deal with child poverty a louder voice than it otherwise might have had.

## Family service targets and the example of Sure Start

A sense of failure was also driven by high outcome expectations that manifested themselves through ambitious targets across family services and their associated evaluations. Sure Start is a prime example.

Sure Start was a broad community programme based in localities with high levels of deprivation assessed on the Jarman Index of Social Disadvantage. For its aspirants it was intended to reduce poverty and to break cycles of disadvantage. Its aim, on the basis of evidence from best practice in early intervention, was:

> To work with parents-to-be, parents and children, to promote the physical, intellectual and social development of babies and young children – particularly those who are disadvantaged – so that they flourish at home and when they get to school, and thereby break the cycle of disadvantage for the current generation of young children. (Barrett, 2007, p 10)

Ambitious measures were used in the evaluation in respect of parenting and children's cognitive, behavioural and social outcomes over a short period of time across the community served, including those who engaged with the programme and those who did not. The results showed some positive gains in relation to non-teenage mothers, but the reverse for teenage mothers.

A subsequent Ofsted review after the service had had a chance to take effect disclosed more positive findings. Family workers were found to offer a valuable service. Parents felt that they had been helped to bond with their children and enabled to learn about child development. Children, particularly those experiencing learning difficulties, were confident and ready for school (James, 2009; Ofsted, 2009). Nevertheless, the outcomes fell short of a level of social change on the scale envisaged and sufficient to satisfy aspiration.

Critiques of Sure Start have referred to ill-defined ambitious aims, with insufficient appreciation of the nature of process and the business of getting the programmes off the ground and embedding them (Rutter, 2006). Target setting and its associated ethos fuels a momentum to deliver demonstrable outcomes within unreasonably short periods of time. The misfortune for Sure Start was that it fell victim to this imperative.

An orientation towards selected outcomes can also detract from necessary attention to, and appreciation of, the role of process. The pressure towards demonstrating outcomes tends to move evaluation concerns away from operational issues, such as bedding in and sustaining supply, which are widely identified to be the point of difficulty for family services (Family and Parenting Institute, 2006). It also short changes the time and process considerations needed for setting up services. Again, this was very evident in the Sure Start initiative (Rutter, 2006). Sure Start involved the establishment and engagement of multiple services in delivering home visits, support to parents and families, services to support good quality play, learning and childcare, primary and community health and social care and access to specialist services. It also specified local consultation in determining aspects of the content and delivery of the programme. Establishing Sure Start took some time, with approximately four years necessary to bed down programmes, a projection that was not made in the rush for outcomes, as reflected in the mistaken offering of premature evaluation findings (Barrett, 2007).

The Sure Start example demonstrates how the perception of family services can suffer because of the scale of government aspiration in relation to their potential impact. Unrealistic outcome expectations were set which did not reflect the limited capacity of family services to effect change. While the broad professional rationale of family services might be to support the upbringing of children and associated family relationships, spin-offs in terms of the educational achievement of young people, closing the achievement gap and the reduction of poverty, are all perceived within 'management speak' and rationale as the outcomes that count. Links there may be. One can cite the evaluation of the Perry Pre-School Project as part of the US Head Start programme, which showed that for every US$1 invested, there was a saving of US$17 to the taxpayer in terms of reduced expenditure on special education, criminal justice costs and lost tax revenue (Schweinhart and Weikart, 1997). But the question remains as to whether across the range of family services the evidence is strong enough, in the light of all the other influences on economic and educational outcomes, to warrant their establishment as organisational aims.

Extravagant aspiration is not appropriate in order to justify investment in family services. When outcomes fall short of unrealistic goals, there is a danger of disincentivising service investors, ranging from the electorate to government and local service commissioners. In addition, the workforce faces the prospect of becoming demoralised. There is also the danger of skews affecting the type of service provided (Henricson, 2007). Targets can skew services away from a sensitive response to need in the round as perceived by professionals, towards the delivery of a limited set of externally selected outcomes. This is a vital issue for personal family services, where flexibility and engaging with the person's self-identified need is required. The risk is that targets rather than the service become the prompt behind management, planning and investment. Particular interests and groups may also come to predominate in evaluation and investment rationales, as has been the case in relation to children's outcomes.

This has been a problem for parenting programmes, where parents' perceptions of the benefits they have received relating to enhanced feelings of support, improved parenting skills and greater self-confidence are generally favourable, even in circumstances where the outcomes for children remain largely unchanged. The evaluation of Home Start, a community programme offering volunteer support in the home, provides an example of this type of finding which placed the promotion of the programme at risk because enhanced child outcomes alone were deemed to be the necessary return on investment (McAuley et al, 2004; Barnes et al, 2006). Should a family support service be found to be detrimental to the welfare of children, then obviously investment should cease. But where there are no such adverse effects, palliative support for families as they bring up children should constitute sufficient justification within a family support model grounded in an ethic of care.

## Reflections

The evidence from these two leading examples of mismanaged target setting within the family policy field underwrites concerns that the target culture encouraged perceptions of New Labour failure. Campaigning and social welfare organisations, and other commentators, undoubtedly contributed to this as they single-mindedly and somewhat simplistically focused on the missing of self-imposed government targets. There was something of an habituation of the progressive agenda with social goods taken for granted and the request for more forming a repetitive refrain; the imposition of elusive and questionable targets fuelled this mind set and narrative of shortcomings.

It is noteworthy that, while most of the strategies for enhancement to family services proposed in *The future of family services* (Henricson, 2002) were indeed implemented, the scale of this achievement passed relatively unsung. It was quite a staggering achievement worthy of rather more accolade than it ever received.

For a future progressive government there are lessons to be learned. If targets are to be set, the logic for their imposition and the feasibility of their attainment should be verifiably established and clearly set out. The full range of possible external influences should be assessed and the dangers of the tendency of targets to skew services and undermine rather than support service processes should also be taken into account.

## The human condition – can it really be changed?

In this section we consider whether New Labour's aspirations in connection with behaviour modification were too great, and whether this, too, predicated an unnecessary sense of failure. In essence the human condition cannot be changed other than through biological evolutionary process. That is a given, but behaviour is susceptible to some manipulation for good, bad or indifferent. The question is whether the New Labour administration expected to change too much too soon.

The extent of our knowledge of how to change human behaviour is in some ways surprisingly limited. Certainly complex population-wide shifts in patterns of behaviour are difficult to predict. The move from habitual obedience to rebellion, or alternatively evolutionary change and the gradual erosion of power bases, constantly take world commentators by surprise; witness the recent Arab Spring, and the changes in the hold of religion as it waxes and wanes.

Single issues offer a greater handle. We have examples of behaviour change, such as the obligatory use of car seat belts, which may be effected swiftly and relatively smoothly. A much slower and organic shift can be seen in smoking patterns. A sustained campaign over decades has resulted in a drop in consumption and the possibility of introducing a smoking ban in public spaces. But nevertheless smoking persists, as does the consumption of illegal drugs.

Research abounds across economic behaviours, social 'nudging', individual psychiatric treatments and more. The essence of the message is that, while there is considerable understanding, human behaviours are susceptible to a host of influences that are hard to weigh up for impact, and there are some ingrained social habits and norms that are hard to budge. Here we look at New Labour's policies on the behavioural change front and consider whether it was over-ambitious; specifically we look at Sure Start, the measures promoting gender equality and the quest to reduce anti-social behaviour.

## Sure Start

The Sure Start aspiration to change behaviours – and consequently outcomes – was a population-wide endeavour, albeit initially within limited geographical boundaries. In the heady days of New Labour when the programme was established, the dimensions and associated difficulties of that aspiration were perhaps not fully appreciated.

A primary issue was the highly intensive nature of the interventions that in the past had been shown to effect change. In his review of the comprehensively evaluated programmes of support for socially disadvantaged families in the US, Gerald Patterson of the Oregon Social Learning Center concluded that a high level of intervention was required to have an impact on children's cognitive and achievement outcomes (Patterson, 1994). He noted Ramey and Ramey's (1992) research that found that home visits of once a week had no effect. Those carried out three times a week had a significant impact, and those conducted five times a week were optimal. The largest effect also related to those interventions that started early and were carried through to the age of eight. The Perry Pre-School Project involved intensive daily classes with the child and regular home sessions with both mother and child (Schweinhart and Weikhart, 2007).

It was the positive results of this intensive provision that influenced the New Labour government to invest in Sure Start. However, the transposition of such individual, highly intensive programmes to function as a population-wide resource was, to say the least, a challenge. Investment on the scale required was simply not possible, or at least not a step that any government was yet prepared to take. Norman Glass, who was at the head of the Treasury initiative establishing Sure Start, made a strong case for greater investment, but failed to win the day (Glass, 2005).

Another difficulty with any parenting and family support programme is the issue of take-up. While popular, there are still parents who do not attend children's centres (Apps et al, 2007), hence the focus by the previous and current governments on the role of outreach work. Parenting programme attrition rates are habitually high, possibly because of the considerable commitment required from participants (Barrett, 2003). Concerns over so called 'hard to reach' families has been the subject of considerable research and service endeavour (Barrett, 2008), and of course the relative costs of investing time and human resources in engaging these families is high. The non-engagement factor is likely to be less for a high profile resource-intensive programme, such as the Perry Pre-School initiative, than for a population-wide facility. Certainly the question of take-up is a significant one for an exercise in shifting patterns of behaviour and outcomes across a social group. The Sure Start evaluation involved a combined assessment of users and those who chose not to take up the offer of services, because the aim of the programme was to change population behaviours, not just the behaviours of participants.

With this combined approach, the numbers not participating contributed significantly to the less than optimal results that emerged from the evaluation, highlighting the considerable difficulties posed by non-engagement.

A third challenge is the length of time needed to have an impact. Certainly the full outcomes of any pre-school initiative will not become evident for a decade or more, although of course there may be earlier positive indications. Parental behaviour change may also take a long time to achieve. If one looks at approaches to discipline, we have come a long way from the punitive methods used in the early 20th century, but it has taken decades and the evolution of attitudes across generations (Henricson and Grey, 2001). Promoting early home learning too is not an easy prospect for parents who may be inadequately educated themselves and not conversant with the methods or notions (Commission on Families and the Wellbeing of Children, 2005).

## Criminal justice

Improving social cohesion through the criminal justice system – and youth justice, in particular – was a high priority for New Labour, much vaunted with the slogan 'Tough on crime, tough on the causes of crime'. The Youth Justice Board, with a prominent chair, Lord Warner, was established, together with local youth offending teams to work intensively with young offenders and their families. Parenting Orders, as we have seen, were a high profile criminal justice tool, as were ASBOs. The public message was that this was something of a crusade for government and, equipped with an evidence base, the measures taken would work. They would provide the answer to what had come to be perceived as 'feral' children, and it was a cause close to the then Prime Minister, Tony Blair's, heart.

Crime is an emotive issue, and its control a primary government function. It is also one of the most difficult aspects of human behaviour to control. Criminology is as uncertain as the science of economic behaviour; prediction is problematic and the evidence contradictory. For example, there is evidence that children at risk of criminal behaviour can be identified at an early stage from factors that range from attention span to their family context with its behavioural traits (Junger-Tas, 1994). There is also evidence that programmes that work with children, if intensive and with a family orientation, can have an impact, even as the child grows older (Patterson, 1994). And yet we have population-wide studies that indicate that non-intervention is more productive than compulsory measures of care. The primary example of this research finding can be seen in the Edinburgh study of youth transitions and crime (McAra and McVie, 2007).

One finding need not necessarily obviate the other, of course. The case might be made that very intensive, clinically based interventions following a closely specified model can effect positive change. However, in the real world of delivering provision to a population, services may not be able to meet these standards, and all the effects of the involvement of a network of welfare agencies and the criminal justice system may present a different story.

There are, too, patterns of behaviour that are beyond the control, or even prediction, of government. Thus, the British Crime Survey shows that, following an escalation of crime levels in the 1960s, 1970s, 1980s and early 1990s, in the 2000s there was a decline in both property and violent crime in England and Wales (Hicks and Allen 1999; Flatley et al, 2010). The Labour Party may like to take credit for this, and yet it was a phenomenon that was international – within the EU crime levels declined between 2003 and 2007 (European Commission, 2010). While the criminal justice system and crime prevention measures may have had a part to play, it might also be reasonable to suppose that the economic stability and prosperity and accumulated social safeguards of that era had left their mark. While overall crime levels remain flat or in decline, there are some indications that the current economic contraction is starting to have an adverse effect, with a 14 per cent increase in the rate of burglary in the latest 2010/11 British Crime Survey figures (Chaplin et al, 2011), and, of course, at the time of writing, the riots of August 2011 have not yet been accounted for in the statistics available.

While crime levels are viewed as a New Labour success, the factors involved in this shift in population behaviours are not fully understood, and the levels of crime reduction have also been insufficient to have an impact on the population's perceptions about the crime rate (Flatley et al, 2010). With such a fluid, slippery situation on the criminality front, governments would be well advised to steer clear of ratcheting up expectations of a victorious war on crime.

## Work–care: gender relations

As we have seen, New Labour invested substantially in financial support, services and legislative stipulation for employers to facilitate a balance between work and care across the gender divide. Alongside providing a route out of poverty, an element of intent was concerned with the promotion of gender equality in the spheres of both work and care. This concern manifested itself in equality-oriented legislation, such as the 2010 Equality Act. The direction of government policy was sufficiently striking to be described by Lewis and Giullari (2005) as promoting the 'adult worker' model with its connotation of equality. There have also been a host of softer measures concerned with supporting fatherhood. Boosting the role of fathers in securing good outcomes for their children was a parallel motive here (O'Brien, 2004), and measures were introduced to engage men with their child's care. *A review of how fathers can be better recognised through DCSF policy* (Page et al, 2008) considered the impact of the various parenting strategies, and found services to be neutral rather than oriented towards engaging fathers. With parenting programmes for men, helplines and even a service campaign 'Think Father', there was a concerted, albeit light touch, effort by government to move services and public attitudes towards an enhanced caring role for fathers. It was a process described by Scourfield and Drakeford (2002) as 'policy optimism'.

Despite the panoply of measures, the road to changing gender relations was a tortuous one, and from the perspective of the egalitarian reformer, less effective than might have been hoped for. Women have been found to make up some 98 per cent of those going part time for family reasons (Barrett, 2004). The traditional division of labour in the home persists for most families (Park et al, 2008). The take-up of parental leave by men continues to disappoint in the UK and elsewhere (Moss, 2008). Overall the evidence suggests that engaging men in equal caring is a long way off, not least because of ongoing traditional attitudes (James, 2009).

The ambivalence of gender related attitudes was perhaps the most difficult issue to address. Thus reforming measures were carried forward by widely voiced egalitarian views, but behaviours belied a stronger attachment to traditional stereotypes than was, and is, generally recognised. The population's aspiration was considerably in advance of the gender-related behaviours described above. In a study by Thompson et al (2005), some 87 per cent of fathers felt as confident as their partners in caring for their child, and 70 per cent that they would like to be more involved in childcare. Williams and Jones (2005) found that some 25 per cent would have liked part-time flexible work and two thirds full-time flexible work when their child was young.

Not only does government have to contend with the complication of the dynamics of ambivalent thoughts and behaviours within individuals and families, it is also in the game of addressing divergent interests associated with the marketplace and organisational practices. Thus we have noted that services are behind strategies in moving towards pro-father rather than gender-neutral provision. In terms of employers, there is also a reluctance to change, with objections raised to legislation that enhances employees' entitlements (OECD, 2008c).

Of the three examples of New Labour's endeavour at shifting behaviour, the sharing of work and care between the genders was given the lightest touch in terms of government promotion and commitment to effecting change. Certainly childcare provision formed part of this package and was widely heralded, but these were facilities for choice, as was the expansion of leave associated with parenthood. The service supports to fatherhood were in evidence, but relatively low key. Broadly it would be fair to say that it was a facilitative approach.

## Reflections

It is noteworthy that of these areas of family policy associated with behaviour management, the one where the New Labour government was rather more reticent about anticipated outcomes was the one concerned with gender relations, which did not constitute one of its internally generated strategies for social enhancement. Rather it was part of the government's engagement with a wider European endorsement of human rights and associated equalities. Of course there was overlap; for example, there was the interface with poverty reduction through female employment in disadvantaged families. Nevertheless, the difference in advocacy and rhetoric was evident.

The other two examples relating to Sure Start and criminal justice were part of a core mission of behaviour change where, as a consequence of conviction and public relations, the government raised expectations to an unrealistic degree. In adopting a more guarded approach in future, some points for consideration emerge.

- First, there is the need to develop a population-wide model for parenting and family support. Rather than a facility that is project or programme-led, a broader conception is needed as to what constitutes realistic provision and anticipated change.
- The model also needs to address the complexities and difficulties of behaviour change that we have witnessed here associated with ingrained behavioural patterns and psychological ambivalence, and the impingement of multiple external factors, including socio-economic environmental issues and divergent interests. The slow nature of behaviour change would need to be accommodated in the model, and, where a span of decades and generations are a likely necessity, this should be acknowledged.

- And finally, a question mark should be placed on the emphasis given to the role of behaviour outcomes in family services. Instead, a facilitative approach should be adopted informed by an ethic of care. Change should not be the price of support; rather support should be provided in response to certain needs. An orientation towards social rights linked to needs would be a more appropriate model.

## Inequality and family policy

These critiques of over-ambitious targets and governmental aspiration for behaviour change lead seamlessly to one of the most substantive of New Labour's misplaced ambitions – the use of family policy to address material inequalities. The proposition discussed is that family policies and services are not suitable as a route to tackle economic inequality. The discussion goes beyond challenges associated with changing human behaviour and relationships, to consider three further critical reasons why family policy might not be the appropriate mechanism for addressing differences in economic and social outcomes.

### Macro-economic scale of the problem

The first concerns the macro-economic scale of the problem. Any argument put forward that the UK's inequality issues are due in a major way to deficits in family relations and children's upbringing should be treated sceptically. Inequality has increased significantly over time despite improvements in educational outcomes and no evidence of a material decline in children's upbringing (Commission on Families and the Wellbeing of Children, 2005). There is also no evidence of a significant difference in parenting in this country compared with other European countries with higher levels of equality.

An analysis of structural issues within the country's framework of operation provides a more compelling explanation. Thus it should be noted that income distribution before state tax and benefits intervention is highly unequal. This is partly attributable to both private and public sector business having come to rely on a low pay model of remuneration for large sections of the population. Income differentials within organisations are high (Hutton, 2011). This level of inequality has been further exacerbated by the development of a finance services-heavy economy with inflated incomes at the top of the scale. The Trades Union Congress (TUC) has commented that income structures have resulted in a substantial proportion of the population on average or low incomes having had little share in the prosperity of the last decade in contrast to higher income groups (Lansley, 2009).

How these structural matters can be addressed is the nub of the inequality debate. It has partially been acknowledged by the current leader of the Labour Party, Ed Miliband, as he has emphasised the need to go beyond redistribution through the tax and benefits system to tackle structural income distribution issues. The introduction of a 'living wage' has been mooted as one measure that might be taken (Miliband, 2011a, 2011b), and government incentives and regulation have been proposed to support 'producers' rather than 'predators' in business, endorsing responsible practice that contributes to the social wellbeing of the nation (Miliband, 2011c). This approach of establishing wage floors and other protection in the face of unequal bargaining power within labour relations has been advocated by economists such as Dolvik (2011) in a new left of centre analysis of the political economy. There has also been Will Hutton's recommendation for transparency and explanations of income differentials within public sector organisations (Hutton, 2011). Other suggestions have been rather more of the ilk of working collaboratively with employers to create high quality jobs (Miliband, 2010). These are helpful but limited and as yet not fully defined proposals to deal with a seriously entrenched systemic fault. Recognising the nature of the problem to be addressed is a step in the right direction, but following that recognition, it is imperative to frame an appropriate policy. The outstanding question is how to respond to inequality in a market economy where it would be counterproductive to forgo the current benefits from a substantial financial sector; the very source of inequality has benefits to offer. It is the twenty-dollar question to which answers are not readily to hand.

However, while this set of root causes may be difficult, if not impossible, to address, they should not be denied or passed over. Resorting to other issues such as improvements in parenting practices and the enhancement of early learning capacity is an evasion. While these are necessary facilities in themselves in terms of enhancing individual and social fulfilment, it would be wholly inappropriate to rely on them to redress core national inequalities.

That is not to say that there are no overlaps. A more educationally and socially skilled workforce may well contribute to some diminution of reliance on benefits. It may even make some contribution to redressing the imbalance in remuneration. A sophisticated multilayered approach is required, but one which does not duck the core role, and failings, of the country's current economic model.

### Inability of family support to have a major impact in the face of inequality

The second point is that the evidence points not only to the secondary role of family policy in shifting patterns of economic inequality, but also to the inability of family support expenditure to counter the negative impact of inequality. According to the Organisation for Economic Co-operation and Development's (OECD) figures, children's outcomes do not reflect the relatively high levels of state spending on children in the UK by the standards of other European countries (OECD, 2011). Children's outcomes in this country are poor, suggesting that state provision is unable to substantially redress the negative effects of structural inequality.

## Moral imperative

The third point of reasoning addresses the issue of how we tackle poverty from an ethical standpoint. There is an argument that from an ethical perspective there is too great an imperative to redress poverty to allow it to be subject to a gradualist approach. The Coalition's response of cutting benefits to already under-resourced welfare recipients runs counter to this ethical stance. So, too, do Frank Field's proposals to freeze inflation increases to certain benefits in order to fund the enhancement of early years facilities (Field, 2010). No one would cavil with the value of investing in early years services. And indeed more childcare may release more mothers to enter the workforce and have a remedial impact on poverty levels – although jobs shortages would probably preclude this. These arguments notwithstanding, of all the financial shifts to make, decreasing in real terms the incomes of families already on the poverty line is morally indefensible.[1]

## Reflections

Rising social inequality has adverse implications for social cohesion, health and a host of other outcomes. International comparisons clearly demonstrate that social benefits accrue to individuals across the income and class spectrum in those societies where inequality is kept to a low level (Wilkinson and Pickett, 2009).

It is critical, then, that governments face up to the issue, albeit that an obvious method of resolution is elusive. What emerge from a review of the predicament are some points of reference. There is, in particular, the need to operate with measures that will have an impact in both the short and long term.

Thus, in relation to the short term, poverty levels need to be reduced in the here and now through tax and benefits redistribution in order for the life chances of children not to be seriously compromised, and in order to sustain standards for all citizens across the age span. In respect of the long term, the structural causes of high levels of inequality need to be addressed, recognising that change will take time and that governments' potential impact may be limited. In developing a strategy it is important for there to be an understanding that the principal player is the market's distribution of income across the population and different income groups. Lost potential at the bottom of the socio-economic scale caused by parenting and education deficits are of less consequence. Certainly their redress would only have an impact at the margins and would not reduce inequality across the population. It would not tackle a highly differentiated rewards system ranging from entrenched levels of low pay to staggering allocations of wealth.

New Labour did appreciate the importance of the short term evidenced through tax and benefits hikes. It saw the introduction of the minimum wage, but this was pitched at a low level, and by and large the administration's modus vivendi was to avoid confrontation with business interests. Instead it placed, or misplaced, its long-term hopes for reducing poverty and inequality on changing behaviour patterns within families with a view to enhancing individual potential to learn and to achieve.

## Child–adult divide

While the New Labour government's creative energies were directed towards a better tomorrow through enhancing children's outcomes, other aspects of family policy took a less prominent place in the scheme of things. There was, perhaps, an over-emphasis on children and insufficient endeavour to see the family in the round, with an important role for government family policy in balancing interests and in sustaining a broad caring function across the generations.

There was, as we have seen in Chapter Two, substantial investment in children's services. In terms of financial support, too, allocations favouring children outstripped those provided to other sections of the community. Benefits for families and individuals without children fell relative to incomes generally – for example, those on Jobseeker's Allowance, Incapacity Benefit and Income Support if living without children (Sutherland et al, 2003).

There was, again as we have seen in Chapter Two, substantial support for pensioners. And there were some examples of broader strategies. A *National action plan on social inclusion 2003-05* was produced as part of an EU initiative, which considered risk across the population including, as well as children, large families, minority ethnic groups, people with disabilities, older people, those living in jobless households, with persistent low incomes and in deprived communities, and intergenerational poverty (DWP, 2003).

But, as noted by Henricson and Bainham (2005), government redistribution policies were still predominantly directed towards addressing children's needs. Child poverty reduction targets dominated anti-poverty publicity. Ministerial strategic statements and the discussion in government documents on social exclusion were largely concerned with the child poverty dimension, and significantly child poverty was the government's primary social exclusion target in the strategy document *Opportunity for all* with its regular progress reports.

There was also, as noted in Chapter Two, some delay in launching a national debate and consultation on the vexed question of the future of social care for older people. Despite widespread anxieties over funding care and evidence of individual hardship, the consultation paper was only issued in 2010. Nevertheless the consultation paper did materialise, and, as we have seen, concerns over the pension age were addressed with increases to the state pension entitlement.

What was missing, however, from both the New Labour government's approach and that of the Coalition, was an overarching view and criteria for the distribution of support across the generations. There was a continued fragmentation between help for older people and help for children. On the service front there was a further split between adult and children's services. The needs of adults in the round, in particular their parenting functions, tended to fall through the net if they were treated within adult health and social care. And the needs of parents and the wider family received insufficient attention within the support provided by children's services (James, 2009). This lack of a cohesive response was acknowledged by the New Labour administration, and a family response was advocated in *Think family* (Social Exclusion Task Force, 2008). However, this service blueprint was largely oriented towards supporting families at risk rather than acknowledging the need to work intergenerationally with families across the board.

The adult–child divide extended to the evaluation of services such as parenting programmes which adopted criteria for success that were oriented largely towards the measurement of children's outcomes. The benefits accruing to parents were of a lesser order (Henricson, 2007). This approach was promoted by the commissioning process which determined child-focused targets, a tendency that has been further reinforced by the Coalition's dalliance with Payment by Results for family services (DfE, 2011b).

## Reflections

New Labour did not take the opportunity of its reappraisal of the state's duties in supporting relationships to develop a comprehensive family policy. Rather, it might be said that its point of engagement and emphasis was in the development of a children's policy. The opportunity was not taken, for example, to debate how government support should be spread across the age span. Poverty in particular is an emotive issue that requires proper debate. Transparent assessment and clearly defined values and associated points of reference are required to steer decisions on resource allocation. Questions need to be asked – and answered – such as whether investment should be led by prevailing poverty levels, or vulnerability, or the potential for making a long-term impact on individual lives and in reducing the intergenerational cycle of disadvantage – or a combination of these. There is a range of moral and practical levels on which these tensions need to be addressed:

The arguments supporting the Government's prioritisation of child poverty are formidable. The UK had one of the highest rates in Europe when the Labour administration came to power (Ruxton and Bennett, 2002). It is also understandable that child poverty might be championed as the acceptable face of economic redistribution. In addition to these two factors, there may be an in-principle argument to be made in favour of weighting social inclusion investment towards the age in life that is likely to derive the greatest long-term benefit from it, with "benefit" defined here in terms of impact on lifetime and intergenerational poverty. With these interlinked arguments, what is perhaps needed is in-depth discussion of the background, principles and policies relating to differentiated investment across age groups. This would provide the opportunity for the development of societal values that set childhood in the context of a lifetime's needs. It would give some transparency to the difficult choices that have to be made and enable a strategy that embraces both a recognition of those choices and the need for their making to be guided by a set of well-aired and understood principles to be pursued. (Henricson and Bainham, 2005, p 46)

As had been discussed, while children were the focal point for the New Labour project, other family members did benefit from an era of plenty and a political ethos favouring safety nets and an element of redistribution. Older people made gains, and social care issues were also a significant governmental concern. What was missing was an across-the-family vision and a policy orientation that looked at the family, its relational interdependency, responsibilities and conflicts in the round.

## Overview

In this chapter we have alluded to the substantial achievements secured as New Labour expanded the role of family policy and developed a host of supports. The thrust of the chapter has, however, been to discuss the difficult directions that were taken and the mistakes made in order to inform the options for a future progressive government.

Problematic targets were examined in some depth in relation to national aspirations, specifically poverty reduction targets, and individual programme development where Sure Start featured. It was found that unrealistic goals had contributed to a sense of failure, and that target setting had the potential to skew service direction inappropriately in favour of certain outcomes and selected population groups at the expense of others. The conclusion drawn was that future governments should only use realistic, verifiable targets that have been determined in a transparent feasibility exercise. Furthermore, targets should only be used sparingly where there are considerable benefits to be had.

The question of unrealistic expectations of behaviour change was considered, and the difficulties encountered across early years upbringing and the Sure Start programme, crime rates and the criminal justice system and gender equality and work–care. The picture did not give rise to despondency across these areas of policy, with advances made on all fronts. The question was whether the expectations were too high and the conclusion was that they were, particularly when associated with the government's core mission. A more guarded approach was advocated for the future, and there were recommendations for the development of a model that could deliver to scale for the population based on a broader conception of what constitutes realistic provision and anticipated outcomes. A move away from operating in the cast of relatively small-scale programmes was proposed. In developing such a realistic population-based approach, the model would need to address the challenges of ingrained behavioural patterns and psychological ambivalence, and the impingement of external factors, including socio-economic environmental issues and divergent interests. The slow nature of behaviour change, in some cases across decades and generations, should be openly acknowledged and factored in. A facilitative rather than a behavioural outcomes approach was advocated, with a significant proposal for greater emphasis to be given to social rights as a response to need.

Possibly the most unrealistic expectation in New Labour's family policy was the belief that poverty could be substantially reduced without addressing the structural inequalities in British society, particularly in relation to income differentials. Acknowledging the scale and intractable nature of the problem, short and long-term measures were needed to have some impact. New Labour had delivered in considerable measure on the short-term dimension with changes to the tax and benefits system. It had also introduced the minimum wage, but this was pitched at a low level, and by and large the administration's modus vivendi was to avoid confrontation with business interests. Instead it placed, or misplaced, its long-term hopes on changing behaviour patterns within families with a view to enhancing individuals' potential to learn and achieve. For the long term the critical point of delivery lies in changing the market's distribution of income across the population. Recent proposals for a living wage, the regulatory promotion of responsible business practice which, inter alia, engages with the needs of employees, and transparency concerning the differentials between top and bottom salaries in public sector organisations – these are all steps in the right direction, but a more radical package of controls may be required to achieve a major impact.

Resources require allocation in the direction of fairness not only in relation to different social groups, but also across the generations. With its focus on child outcomes, New Labour did not engage in debate or transparent consideration about how resources should be apportioned across the age span. While other family members, particularly older people, did benefit from an affluent era and a government with a redistributive slant, what was missing was a cohesive family policy that had as its central function the promotion of family wellbeing in the round, informed by an understanding of families' relational interdependency, responsibilities and conflicts.

In this analysis of *what was wrong*, some significant pointers for future curtailment and future action have emerged. In the next chapter we expand on these to voice some thoughts for the scope and orientation of the next phase of development.

## Note

[1] Comparison with a country such as Sweden, which spends more on services relative to benefits than the UK (OECD, 2011), would be inappropriate because Sweden's pre-benefit income distribution is markedly more equal than that which pertains in this country.

# SIX

# Looking to the future

In this chapter the argument shifts from what has been to what the future should hold in store. The conceptual foundations for the development of family policy are mooted, and there is an assessment as to what a realistic and purposeful policy would be for the next phase of progressive government.

Having examined what was good and what was wrong with family policy over the last 15 years under New Labour and the Coalition, the argument now changes gear. Learning the lessons from this retrospective, it moves on to develop a structure for family policy so that it is less reactive to other government agendas, less fragmentary and in possession of greater cohesion and *raison d'être* sufficient to enable the term 'family policy' to be legitimately used. The framework proposed is informed by an endeavour to manage the tensions that impact on family life, rather than by expectations of securing major social, relational or behavioural improvements.

## Concept of family policy

There was a discussion in Chapter One of the fluid and malleable nature of family policy. Fertility issues were cited as a major political goal in a number of European countries, and the review of politics and the family in recent years in the UK has shown how ambitions to change economic and social relations have been routed through this policy field. The case has been made that this is not a legitimate approach. Particular interest groups may prevail in these circumstances and, as we have seen, too many and too great expectations may be loaded onto an area of policy that cannot deliver. Policy to support family relations has its own *raison d'être*. It may have moderate outcome expectations, but it is nevertheless essential, and it needs a conceptual 'ring fence' to enable it to function effectively.

Family policy is about familial relationships and facilitating these. The very definition of family, even in the tight context of the state's perspective, is about personal relationships. Set out in Chapter One, it is reiterated here as an important reminder and point of reference for the purpose of developing a new family policy framework.

A social unit where there is a legal or customary expectation by the state of unremunerated family support and caring, specifically:

- a legally recognised parent child relationship (whether biological or social) and/or
- a legally recognised adult couple relationship.

These relationships are central to social being. And yet they are also precarious. Highly dependent on trust, they are subject to frequent fracture and breach of that trust. They are the place where the full gambit of emotions and behaviours interact, often at a high level of intensity because of the proximity and intrusive nature of family life. They are the place where the vexed ambivalence of human emotions is played out. They reflect the acute contradictions of the human psyche. Darwin identified empathy, largely derived from the parent–child relationship, and aggressive self-assertion as the main protagonists in this drama (Darwin, 1871). That indeed may not be enough. There are sadistic elements, so often overlooked because of their inexplicable nature and the discomfort they cause. To this mix should be added the heady brew of sex and romantic love. There are power relations and the search for collective security versus individual fulfilment across a host of material and less material domains. It is against this highly fraught and volatile background that the essential role of caring takes place, which requires state support and regulation; there is dependency and there is vulnerability that requires protection – again, state support and regulation. The complexities of family life as described here demonstrably require a state function that can both support and regulate from the perspective of a full understanding of family operations. It is this role of reconciling and managing the tensions of family relations in the interests of family wellbeing that has perhaps not been fully identified or articulated by either the New Labour or Coalition governments. It needs articulation and conceptual development. Management of family life is critical and should form the principal component of family policy.

We have witnessed the limitations and risks associated with the use of family policy as a means of securing a shift in broad socio-economic relations. A reformulated model is required, and here an option that refocuses direction in four significant ways is explored.

## Family wellbeing

First, family wellbeing should be at the centre of family policy; that should be its purpose. The model would endorse support and control measures that promote family wellbeing. It would emphasise the impact of public policy on families rather than treating families as a tool of public policy for ends that are other than the direct enhancement of family wellbeing. By way of example, measures to enhance the degree to which families can choose the number of children which they have would fall within this definition, while measures to encourage or discourage fertility with a view to controlling population levels would not. A further example relates to redistribution and the reduction of inequalities. The introduction of a range of redistributive economic, social and environmental measures commensurate with the scale of the challenge with the intended outcome of promoting family wellbeing as well as other social goods, such as health and community cohesion, would fall within the definition. Investment in the improvement of family educative and relational behaviours with disproportionate and unrealistic expectations of breaking patterns of social immobility and inequality, on the other hand, would not.

The thrust of this aspect of the model is largely about motivation. It is important and not to be dismissed as an esoteric discussion point. Motivation that is about family wellbeing will take family policy in an appropriate direction. It will prevent the discrediting of services because they do not deliver outcomes defined by other agendas. Thus, for example, long-term public savings are not the primary objective of a family policy with family wellbeing as its rationale; an ethic of care is a more appropriate value. In these circumstances supports that give comfort to parents, even if they do not enhance children's long-term economic outcomes, would be deemed worthwhile.

This different orientation for family policy would enable the lessons learned in Chapter Five in relation to unrealistic outcomes-driven targets to be more readily applied. The sparing use of fully assessed, realistic targets, and a guarded approach in expectations of behaviour change, would be more easily accommodated within a family policy agenda formulated exclusively with family wellbeing as its purpose rather than external drivers for change. Discipline would still be required to balance aspiration with realism, but the policy dynamic would reduce the pressure to achieve the unachievable.

How, then, should the best interests of families – family wellbeing – be appropriately addressed in the development of public policy? The means of establishing our understanding of family wellbeing have to be identified as a preliminary requirement for planning, implementation and monitoring purposes, and administrative structures to oversee delivery are also pertinent.

The development of a set of family wellbeing indicators would provide a definition of family wellbeing sufficient to equip government with a workable framework. While human rights may provide the broad definition of core entitlements for individuals within families, they require conceptual amplification. A tool could be developed, drawing on the new interdisciplinary studies of the nature of family wellbeing incorporating human rights values. In a recent review of wellbeing measures, Wollny et al (2010) identified the potential to draw indicators from across a range of domains – physical, social, economic and psychological – to develop a set of national family wellbeing indicators. The set should include subjective as well as objective measures, for example, feelings about family relationships (subjective) and levels of household income (objective).

The indicators would differ from the wellbeing exercise currently being undertaken by the Office for National Statistics (2011a) on behalf of the Coalition government in having a specific family dimension covering relationships across the generations in the context of family life. They would offer a particular focus on family functioning, the quality of relationships, caring, morality as cast within families and mental health issues. They would move away from reliance on the household as an economic unit for measurement, to the family caring relationship network, with a definition of 'family' as set out at the beginning of this chapter. A consultative approach might be adopted, drawing on a tool developed in Ireland for measuring child wellbeing, but adapted to be applicable to the intergenerational family. The Irish *State of the nation's children* report is based on a set of indicators of children's wellbeing that is both comprehensive and nuanced in terms of the issues covered, and inclusive in that it draws on a multiplicity of research and consultative exercises. The broad reach of wellbeing is recognised encompassing a range of disciplines. The following expansive definition of wellbeing was used to guide the exercise.

> Health and successful functioning (involving physiological, psychological and behavioural levels of organisation), positive social relationships (with family members, peers, adult care givers, and community and societal institutions, for instance, school, faith and civic organisations), and a social ecology that provides safety (eg freedom from interpersonal violence, war and crime), human and civil rights, social justice and participation in civil society. (Andrews et al, 2002, p 3)

This definition was used because of the inclusion of many different dimensions of children's lives along with formal and informal supports, thereby presenting a whole child perspective.

Using the Delphi technique, an advisory group of experts from different disciplinary backgrounds undertook three exercises:

- examination of some 80 international, national and regional indicator sets;
- a review of current data availability in Ireland;
- consultation with children.

These were followed by three rounds of questionnaires to stakeholders; the expert group reviewed the results of each round and with this information, inputted into the next interrogation. This incremental investigative approach meant that the resulting indicator set was both sophisticated and in possession of widespread ownership credentials (National Children's Office of Ireland, 2005).

The proposed family wellbeing indicators would require refreshing regularly, possibly every three to five years as a consultative document, to accommodate changes in social mores, advancing a consensual approach, but always within human rights parameters.

As a 'living' instrument the indicators would provide a guide and litmus test for family policy across those government departments that inevitably have a role to play in its promotion. The possibility of family impact statements being required in respect of current and prospective legislation with the indicator set as a point of reference should also be explored as a means of focusing attention on families' needs across the range of pertinent government functions. The Coalition government is formulating family checks for legislation following the August 2011 riots and emergent anxieties over family functioning (Cameron, 2011). These are undeveloped at present, but it may be anticipated that they will have a relatively narrow focus on behavioural issues.

There are precedents for such impact statements, some of which have operated more effectively than others. Thus, following the 1998 Human Rights Act and the 2010 Equality Act, human rights and equalities are a point for consideration in developing legislation and administration in the UK, and when government or other administrative bodies fall short, a vocal opposition has been able to point to the deficiencies and to seek redress (see, for example, UK WBG, 2011). Family impact statements were introduced in Australia in 2005, but without constituting a sufficiently tight point of reference to ensure that compliance was as meaningful as it might have been (Australian Government, Department of the Prime Minister and Cabinet, 2009). The linking of a set of indicators to impact assessment requirements would provide a tighter and more muscular implementation framework.

A further contribution to supporting the totality of family wellbeing in the mind set of government would be provided by the institution of a regular review of the proportionate allocation of national resources across the generations. Addressing family wellbeing in a comprehensive fashion spanning the full range of interests that it comprises, in particular intergenerational interests, has been identified as one of the major deficits of the New Labour and Coalition governments' dealings with families. It begs a multilayered response, part of which would entail some rationalisation of the government department bidding process. Moving on from fragmentary responses will not be easy, and a change in government culture and procedures away from competitive departmental bidding towards a more cohesive approach would be required.

A central development function would be needed to motor and oversee these processes, and for the purpose of strategic thinking and operations across departments, a central function within government, possibly located in the Cabinet Office, would have more power than an external watchdog such as the EHRC.

## Managing tensions via rights

The second consideration relates to the management of tensions. We have reflected on the split in families between caring and individualism, even selfishness, and the existence of divergent as well as supportive interests. The tensions are numerous – between individuals, across generations and interests, and between families and the state. Their reconciliation is one of the primary functions of family policy, and a brief exploration of their scope gives some indication of the importance of addressing this reconciliatory role effectively.

In respect of internal family relationships, tensions are subject to a host of regulations that apply across society relating to crime, civil law and more. But families do have specific regulations pertaining to their unique tensions associated with adult couple and parent–child relationships. This is the stuff of family law and child protection. The management of these specific tensions is a major component of family policy.

Material loss and gain constitutes the essence of many societal tensions and they have a substantial presence in family relations. On the allocation of the nation's resources front we have the question as to how resources are distributed across gender, parental status and generation. There are continual and inevitable tensions as to the degree to which investment should be directed towards children or the older generation, and the distribution of parental financial support to mothers or fathers, and the financial call of adults without children. The list of tussles is endless.

Then there is a substantial tug of war between the state and the family in fulfilling caring functions. In terms of financial support, there are financial obligations within families and between the state and families. That parents should have some level of responsibility for the financial maintenance of their children is unquestioned and internationally applicable. This may be through work and/or application for child-related benefits, and then the subsequent deployment of these resources for the maintenance of the child. This responsibility is encapsulated in Article 27 of the 1989 UN Convention on the Rights of the Child: 'The parents or others responsible for the child shall have primary responsibility to secure, within their abilities and financial capacity, the conditions of living necessary for the child's development'. The state also has responsibility: 'State parties, in accordance with national conditions and with their means, shall take appropriate measures to assist parents and others responsible for the child to implement this right'.

Governments have sought to bolster the financial viability of families through supporting families on the one hand, and reinforcing parental responsibilities, for example, through work requirements, on the other. However complementary these two routes may be, there is an obvious difference between them that requires clarification in order to minimise the tension.

Financial support by the state and families is not the only locus of dual support responsibilities. Care in kind also features. For example, health, education and social care for older people, and other advisory and therapeutic family facilities all feature. The parameters of the state's role and families' own responsibilities across all these areas is a constant drama, from the creation of legislation to the process of practical daily living.

And tensions move in two directions, between families wanting more support from the state on the one hand, and wanting less on the other, with resentments towards overbearing state intervention. There is a fundamental strain between the state's role in supporting parents and the scope of the parents' caring responsibilities and associated autonomy (Henricson, 2003).

Tensions within families and in relation to the state combine and can be seen in higher profile in relation to child protection. Here the interests of the child differ from those of other family members. The crossover between supporting a family and removing a child into care – with all the child protection measures in between – is one of the most difficult balancing acts for state intervention.

In the intervention sphere there is yet a further division between the interests of the wider community and the operation of family relationships, particularly in relation to criminal justice matters. The high levels of child incarceration and the low age of criminal responsibility, and the imposition of Parenting Orders, are all examples of where the balance has moved in favour of the community. Again, there is a difficult balance to be struck.

### Rights

One possible method of navigating this complexity of tensions would be to move towards a rights approach. Rights can act as a relatively transparent arbiter between individuals in families, and families and the state. Rights dimensions include matters associated with safety, social protection, access to family life, caring and financial security.

Rights provide a mechanism for handling individual and collective interests openly and relatively fairly. Under a rights model there are expectations of a balance of interests, a balance that would be more vulnerable under a welfare model where there is a high level of discretion in government investment.

Rights can be civil, largely synonymous with freedoms, or social, largely synonymous with entitlements. The two sorts are, of course, closely linked. Thus minimum living standards of food, rest and housing may be associated with the right to freedom from inhuman and degrading treatment, and, as we have seen, the right to respect for a family life is undermined if the requisite social supports are not available.

> Abandoning the conventional dichotomy can give us a clearer picture of the nature and range of human rights and allow us to see much more clearly their manifold interrelationships. Our lives – and the rights we need to live them with dignity – do not fall into largely separate political and socioeconomic spheres. (Donnelly, 2003, p 32)

Rights have been the subject of considerable misunderstanding. They have been conceived of as adversarial and, when associated with the pursuit of parents' rights, as undermining concern for children's needs (Williams, 2004). This negative perspective does not take into account the reality of children's rights or the role of rights in regulating different interests in family life, which is essential for the ordered division of resources and the protection of children after couples separate.

Crucially, it also fails to address the role of rights in protecting families in relation to the support they receive from the state. Rights regulate to some degree state power to grant or deny support. They are concerned with people's critical needs, a universal core associated with health, wellbeing and the opportunity for fulfilment. The significance of welfare and behavioural outcomes should of course not be discounted. They should form part of a family services strategy, but as a subsidiary to rights, which should be given greater centrality in a new family policy model.

Rights have been lambasted most recently for undermining responsibilities (Cameron, 2011). Partly the result of a moralistic lashing out of blame following the riots and fears of an unworthy underclass, this negativism has also been associated with criticisms of the 1998 Human Rights Act as being over-protective of the right to respect for family life in the context of immigration (May, 2011). Emotive responses aside, there are misconceptions about rights, with a false dichotomy perceived between rights and responsibilities. Rather than being opposites, they are in fact closely complementary. An individual and collective person's rights imply responsibilities for delivery and a symbiotic process in the give and take and interdependence of social relations. From the negotiation of rights, responsibilities emerge. The process is one of transparency and open negotiation of individual and social interests and associated obligations.

The transition of broad human rights to the particularity of entitlements and administrative and legal interpretation is a challenge. Nevertheless the evidence since the introduction of the European Convention on Human Rights is that it can be achieved, and that the process has contributed to the enhancement of support and protection in the family policy field.

Thus the Convention and the Human Rights Act have had an impact on services standards for citizens with a disability (Munby, 2006). In relation to family support, the right to respect for a private and family life contained in these instruments, and the provisions promoting the best interests of the child in the 1989 UN Convention on the Rights of the Child, have given impetus to expectations that adults with disabilities should be supported in their parenting role so that their children are not removed unnecessarily into local authority care, and this is borne out in case law developments (Olsen and Tyers, 2004).

A further example, discussed in Chapter Three, is the duty that has fallen to local authorities to keep families together. The article underwriting respect for family life has informed significant case law development in relation to the provision of family support services (Henricson and Bainham, 2005).

The EHRC has provided an additional dimension in focusing concerns over human rights violations across areas of social policy without the restrictions of a case law approach. A report revealing the inadequacy of social care for older people is one example of the scope of this type of work (EHRC, 2011). The Commission offers a point of pressure sufficient to shift some aspects of social policy. Human rights and equalities impact statements have a similar function in being able to bring pressure to bear in relation to prospective legislation.

The interface between human rights case law and family policy has been explored in depth in *The child and family policy divide* (Henricson and Bainham, 2005). In addition to the state's obligation in terms of family support, case law is shown to have a considerable locus across the clash of interests within families in relation to children's education, post-separation contact arrangements, adoption procedures and more. The process of weighing up the claims and counter-claims in an open and proportionate fashion is examined with the conclusion drawn that rights' processes, because of their legal context and recognition of interests across citizen groups, provide a transparent and fair means of recognising inherent differences and problematic power relations.

In terms of the European Convention on Human Rights, brought into domestic legislation by the Human Rights Act, particularly pertinent articles include: Article 8(1), 'everyone has the right to respect for his private and family life, his home and his correspondence'; Article 3, which relates to freedom from torture and inhuman and degrading treatment; Article 6, the right to a fair hearing, which has procedural implications for childcare processes; and Protocol 1, Article 2, which provides a right to education. These rights cover a broad spectrum of issues associated with relationships within and between families, government and the wider community.

Transparency is required to promote the collective and individual interests associated with families in a balanced and fair way. A clear, open policy is needed on the relationship between the state and the family, and on the relationship between older dependents, children, parents and other adults. Intergenerational and intergender interests need to be reconciled. That is a role for government, guided by a set of principles that adhere to international human rights. While there are hurdles to be overcome, rights do have the benefit of being able to arbitrate openly and fairly between individuals in families and between families and the state. However, human rights as defined by the Convention and the Act require amplification, and while there is evidence of this having been achieved through case law, to date this has tended to be fragmentary and responsive to single cases brought to courts by individuals. The creation of the EHRC and equalities and human rights impact statements have helped in going beyond individual case orientation and are consequently suggestive of a way forward. Greater cohesion and scope suited to the execution of a family policy might be achieved through amplification via the proposed set of family wellbeing indicators and the development of associated entitlements. There would also be links with the family impact statements, resource reviews and the central family policy government function previously discussed. In order to be functional, the model developed should be confined to core expectations capable of population-wide delivery, taking on board the lessons learned in Chapter Five concerning over-ambitious aspirations.

### Responsibilities

Running in tandem with a clearer definition of rights should be a clearer specification of the corresponding responsibilities of the state and individuals to deliver these rights vis-à-vis families. There is a strong case to be made for greater clarity and openness in our expectation of responsibilities. The word is bandied around, but largely from the perspective of decrying the state of the world today versus the past, much as humanity has done down the ages. In fact responsibilities are essential ingredients in the business of social functioning. They fall to individuals and the state in their role of caring and supporting families. It has been extensively argued that society would benefit from greater clarification of these roles than currently pertains.

Here we draw attention to two examples of individual family responsibilities which dovetail with the responsibilities of the state and which are widely recognised as suffering from a lack of definition. Constituting significant deficit areas and the very crux of the family's support function, they are the caring obligations of parent to child, and the caring obligations of adult child to parent.

**Adult children supporting their parents**

The role of the adult child in caring for an elderly parent is undefined in law in this country, but the moral obligation is significantly in evidence. Indeed it is a role without which the country's system of elder care would seriously falter. There are, however, examples of legal obligations in other jurisdictions. In France 'l'obligation alimentaire' places an obligation of basic material maintenance on the adult child if the parent is suffering from significant deprivation, and a similar obligation exists in Singapore. There have recently been calls for legal obligations to be adopted in the UK; Baroness Deech, a family lawyer, made the case for a caring duty in a highly publicised address to Gresham College. 'In return for all that grandparents do, should there not be an obligation to keep them, and to keep parents, and reciprocate the care that was given by them to children and grandchildren in their youth?' (Deech, 2010).

Undoubtedly the process of defining familial responsibilities would require in-depth consideration of the practicalities of caring obligations. There would be matters such as the interplay of financial support and care in kind, the fair division of responsibility between siblings, and the relationship with the obligations of the state. What is or is not enforceable would come into play. It may be that a communal solution may be preferred with older people supported through their entitlement from the state, and support from families only constituting a genuinely optional addition. If familial responsibilities are preferred, there are a range of options for consideration, for example, a possible interchange of financial support and care in kind, and means testing.

The process would be complex, but no more than other splits between state and family responsibilities, and the difficulties are in existence – whether defined or undefined. Evasion through not defining roles is irresponsible, and the current uncertainty is a major failing, with families not knowing the extent of their responsibilities and anticipated support. It is also inequitable in that the division of responsibility falls unfairly between siblings, with chance circumstance, such as location and negotiation skills, having a very significant impact on outcomes.

### Parents supporting their children

The lack of a coherent legal definition of the role of parents vis-à-vis their children has been widely reflected on as a point of concern in socio-legal discourse. In a review of the relationship between *Government and parenting*, Henricson (2003) assessed the implications of the English Law Commission's decision in 1998 not to propose a statement of parents' rights and responsibilities because it considered that the complexity of the process was prohibitive. Henricson disagreed with the Commission's decision, noting that as a consequence, the legal incidence of parenthood has had to be pieced together from multiple sources, an approach that undermines transparent government. Transparency is a significant matter for parents who should be aware of the matters that may prompt state intervention such as the taking of children into care. The ongoing rumblings about parents falling short of ill-defined responsibilities are also indicative of the need for greater clarity as to what we as a society are asking of parents.

Following the logic of this argument and drawing on a range of instruments both domestic and international, Henricson developed a possible code for parenthood for public debate. It encompassed a set of principles supported by guidance intended to:'provide an instrument of sufficient detail to be meaningful, without being an over didactic, invasive imposition of legal regulation' (Henricson, 2003, p 94). The duties concerned maintenance, education, safety, physical and emotional nurture, the humane promotion of pro-social behaviour and respect for children's rights and associated agency. Options of establishing the code as guidance or as a statutory instrument linked to the 1989 Children Act were mooted, with public information and clarity being the object rather than the criminalising of parents.

## Changes in social mores – a sensitive response

The third proposition to be considered is that a distinguishing dimension of family policy should be its capacity to respond flexibly and sensitively to shifts in moral perceptions and behaviours. Changes in this sphere are pertinent to all aspects of human relations and their interface with government policy. They have their place in determining directions across foreign policy, environmental concerns and economic and social welfare matters; politics and morality are intertwined. The contention here, however, is that the intimate morality associated with family relations are at the root of society's wider moral fabric. Changes to this morality are consequently of particular significance. They also require a high degree of sensitivity from government if policy directions are not to be too lax to offer protection and order, or too directional so as to be repressive.

One of the considerable achievements of the Labour movement since the 1960s has been to facilitate the expression of liberation in family and intimate relationships. It has enhanced equality between the sexes, been inclusive and enabled greater choice in ways of living through, for example, providing the facility of civil partnerships to support same-sex relationships; preventing discrimination between different family forms; and promoting children's rights and avenues of self-expression and policy influence.

Developing a government disposition and structure to gauge and accommodate changing perspectives would enable the social liberalism of the past decade to be preserved and built on. There are highly sensitive issues needing attention, such as the question of assisted dying where the law is out of kilter with trends of thought within the population. Then there is the relationship between the generations, duties of care, the role of self-fulfilment versus familial responsibilities – these are all matters of moment.

This responsive approach is also needed across the whole gamut of family policy in guiding the state's family support function. It should underwrite the development of family wellbeing indicators and the interplay and scope of rights, and associated expectations of government.

Managing the tensions in social relations between state and individuals and between individuals themselves is highly fraught in relation to families where there are sensitivities and continual changes in perceptions and behaviours. Families are where patterns of morality evolve, a process that is not a straightforward projection of what is right and wrong, and governments need to strike a balance between influence and responsiveness – and to do so in open discussion.

The provision in these proposals for emphasis on rights-based governance and the development of family wellbeing indicators drawing on a national consultation would provide a transparent and evolutionary framework. However, the fluidity of morality and enhanced understanding of the issues at stake in a changing environment where different traditions and perspectives are in play suggest that an additional facility may be required.

## Moral behaviour, families and the state

It is within families that formative relationships are experienced, that in turn have an impact on multiple social relations. Attitudes to sexual, gender and intergenerational relations become ingrained from an early age. The role of religion, civic duty, the scope of mutual responsibility, of conformity and of individual free will, all come from the mould of early intimacies. There is, too, the development of the human psyche and the interplay of the brain and behaviour, of which we are becoming increasingly aware through advances in neuroscience. Moral behaviour and its formulation is a highly complex and slippery field that does not operate from an agreed, stable endorsement of a particular stance. It has instead been the subject of discourse and questioning through the centuries. There have been revelatory approaches, largely associated with religious experience, and cogently argued secular moral philosophies. Taking on board this diversity, we look here at the issue through analysis of the evidence of human behaviour – evolutionary interpretations.

Darwin took the view that there was a universal direction to morality. He considered that it had arisen in humanity because of a combined capacity for memory, intelligent thought and language, and that it was the result of a need to order and prioritise impulses so as to avoid regret or succumbing to one at the expense of another. Darwin described the array of instincts, needs and behaviours: from hunger and anger, shame and fear of approbation, to the parent–child relationship. He nevertheless focused on two principal drivers – social instincts and innate aggression – and deemed the social instincts to be prioritised within morality because they provide longer-term satisfaction (Darwin, 1871).

There is, however, a different interpretation that is pertinent here which suggests that the prioritisation of the social instincts is by no means a given. While elements of deferred gratification in humans are widely recognised, gratification that satisfies the ego in ways not necessarily to do with social instincts may be pursued as a long-term goal. Examples include sustaining interests of the mind, the pursuit of the arts and the acquisition of status symbols. Then there is the assuagement of hunger through long-term forward planning. Critically, there is also the fulfilment of the emotional drivers of the ego in relation to sexuality which can involve sustained action contravening the social mores of the group: homosexuality, adultery and desertion. These and many other examples can be given of the pursuit of the meaningful life that involves a considered prioritisation of aspects of the ego that are not to do with social instincts. The fulfilment of other needs can produce long-term satisfaction, and if denied can result in emotional, intellectual or physical crippling. Indeed it has been the denial of these egotistical needs that has caused some thinkers to deprecate rigid codes of conduct in favour of a liberated ego (Midgley, 1984).

It is even questionable as to whether social instincts are necessarily the prime purpose of morality. Might not morality be the management of different emotional and cognitive pulls within the human psyche, with the social instincts being one, but not necessarily the dominant, pull? The evidence suggests that morality may in reality be associated with the interplay of needs: egotism and even cruelty, as well as pro-social empathy.

Shifts in morality – episodic change and movement over time – provide one of the clearest indications of morality as the tool endeavouring to hold the reins between the muddled drivers of the human psyche. These include major shifts in sexual mores, intergenerational relations, filial duties, expectations of self-sacrifice and self-realisation, and obedience and challenge to authority within the family, the community and the state.

The complexity of human motives, their tensions and contradictions, is considerable. They go beyond the dichotomy between sociability and competition. They cross a range of short and long-term impulses, some innate, some cultural and some that, despite the advances of behavioural science, we do not yet understand. Morality is a significant player in the maelstrom, not as a simple promoter of social instincts, but rather as a manager of the human condition (Henricson, in preparation).

The difficulties, subtleties and changes in the development and application of morality exist in relation to both interpretations – both Darwin's approach that aligns morality to the social instincts, and the alternative contention that a broader range of impulses and motives are accommodated by moral codes. It is that propensity to change in the realm of human thought and culture that points to the role of public debate on the constructs and currency of morality and ethics. To facilitate, and indeed boost, that role, a body with the purpose of providing a focus for the investigation, reflection and debate of issues of moment in the sphere of ethics, morality and relationships might be established.

Preference should probably be given to an institution distanced from government. Open debate would be prejudiced by too close a connection with any political position, or with an establishment civil service. Rather than having a directly supportive function in relation to government, the 'body' would engage with 'difference'. It would stimulate change, thereby diminishing the potential for established morality and culture to ossify and act as a force for repression, out of kilter with developing thinking and popular sentiment.

Sartre and D.H. Lawrence are examples of leading thinkers who rejected what they perceived as the stultifying nature of the morality of their day and its suppressing of individual fulfilment (Midgley, 1984). Kenneth Clark (1969) captured the value of opposition and difference in providing the catalyst for progressive human intercourse in his analysis of *Civilisation*. The opposition Clark referred to was between the state and the church, which was pivotal to the development of Western Europe over centuries. The proposals put forward here do not have pretensions on this scale, but they do derive from the same stream of thought that challenging debate contributes to a culture and moral framework that has a progressive dynamic.

What form the 'body' might take is also a matter for consideration. It would need a well-known identity that had significant currency among the wider public in order to be able to act as a stimulus for public debate. Placing it in academia where discussion may take place without wider engagement would perhaps not be the most appropriate route. While academic analysis would be highly relevant, topicality and policy orientation would also be needed. A single organisation or a network distributed across existing institutions would both be options.

## A new 'family wellbeing' typology

Policy analysis tools both reflect and reinforce policy approaches and priorities. This is certainly the case in family policy, and for this reason the fourth proposal for future steps is the development of a new typology for assessing national family policies. Comparisons with other countries should form part of the ongoing review envisaged here, not only as a broader point of reference, but also because such an analytical function recognises and supports interconnected family policies across national boundaries. While there is obviously a global relevance, the governmental and legislative links via EU and Council of Europe institutions makes comparisons at a European level particularly pertinent. A new typology might also fill a deficit in comparative tools, a deficit that may to some extent be holding back our understanding and the consequent impetus behind family policy.

The European FAMILYPLATFORM, following its review of family research across Europe, concluded that the current typologies available were not satisfactory. They do not deliver a framework for the understanding of what is a fast moving government function, where traditional fits of welfarism versus liberalism, familialisation and de-familialisation, gender equality versus inequality, and the North–South European models of family policy fail to adequately describe and understand the nature of developments (Blum and Rille-Pfeiffer, 2010). There has been growing convergence in the types of family services provided alongside growing fluidity in the socio-political framework of states, rendering it more difficult to slot them into traditional categories. The EU provides close policy links for member states that have not been fully accounted for. It has also expanded, and there are now multiple historical perspectives within its membership. Particular confusions have been thrown up by the post-communist East European accession states that defy easy definition as each develops its own particular socioeconomic political stance. To all this must be added the economic downturn, with crisis points reached in growing numbers of European states; there is the potential for imminent social change of differing dimensions across the continent. A full understanding of the scale and fall-out from this change in European fortunes eludes us at this point in time.

Given this melee of change over time, a typology is needed that can hold and has a contribution to make for the foreseeable future, and which has an expectation of movement. The typology should also endeavour to reflect some of the breadth of family policy across a variety of policy streams. Typologies to date have tended to focus on a limited range of issues, such as state social welfare, gender equality and the offer of care choices. And significantly the focus has largely been on the family context for the upbringing of children, rather than an intergenerational approach being taken. Some attempts have been made to conjoin strands, such as the broadening of Esping-Andersen's classification of social welfare systems to include a gender dimension (Blum and Rille-Pfeiffer, 2010). Hantrais (2004) has arguably gone the furthest in taking a broad perspective through her analysis of the historical trends that have contributed to European family policy structures. However, levels of family wellbeing do not feature in her analysis, which is essentially an essay in governmental and administrative structure.

What is lacking in this suite of typologies is coherence in that the policy elements chosen, while pertinent to families, appear somewhat fragmentary. They reflect different aspects of policy that affect families, but not an identifiable entity of family policy. They also leave out the critical over-rider of human rights. The limitation of these analytical tools, perhaps, is that they reflect the predicament of family policy, which is that it has tended to be the object of other government agendas, and is consequently analysed from that perspective; single issues, albeit of major dimensions such as the role of the welfare state, tend to inform the analytical tools.

Is the development of a typology that goes beyond this reflection of the reality of current political operation feasible? Could it indeed provide a useful conceptual shift? The following elements of a future typology draw on the family policy framework developed in this book. They are floated here for consideration.

The typology would be one that operates on two levels with two separate but linked overarching aims. The first would be to assess the degree to which countries have a comprehensive family policy with the object of enhancing family wellbeing. The second would be to assess the degree to which countries are attaining standards of family wellbeing.

In relation to the first, the following specifications for measurement are proposed:

- a comprehensive family policy that spans interests both aligned and divergent across the generations;
- a family wellbeing and reconciliation of familial tensions orientation for family policy;
- operation within a framework of civil and social rights;
- engagement of the public in determining the parameters of family wellbeing and expected standards.

The following types of research questions might be asked to determine the degree to which a country fulfils these specifications.

### *A comprehensive family policy that spans interests both aligned and divergent across the generations*

- Does the country have a specific family policy?
- What is its scope? Does it span aligned and divergent interests across the generations?

- How far is it integrated into the fabric of government in terms of effectual power, including matters such as governmental institutions and the scrutiny of legislation?

### *A family wellbeing and reconciliation of familial tensions orientation for family policy*

- Does the country's family policy specify the promotion of family wellbeing and the reconciliation of familial tensions as its core, overarching aim?
- How far is this aim the driver of family policy in reality?
- Have a set of family wellbeing indicators been developed?

### *Operation within a framework of civil and social rights*

- Does the country's family policy specify a civil and social rights dimension?
- If it does specify such a dimension, what is its scope?
- Where there is no specification in relation to family policy, is there nevertheless a significant civil and social rights dimension to measures that have an impact on families?
- How far is there transparency and clear definition of families' and the state's respective caring responsibilities?

### *Engagement of the public in determining the parameters of and expected standards relating to family wellbeing*

- How far is the public consulted in determining the parameters of and expected standards relating to family wellbeing?
- How far has the government undertaken measures to stimulate public debate on morality and ethical matters that affect the family?

The second level of the typology concerns the degree to which standards of family wellbeing are being met and the development of a set of European family wellbeing indicators. One of the major difficulties in making pan-European comparisons relates to inconsistent measures across the full range of data collection on families and their wellbeing (Rupp et al, 2011). This hampers collective and comparative review of the impact of different policy measures introduced by both domestic and international government. A set of internationally endorsed indicators of family wellbeing would provide, at the lowest level of expectation, the means by which governments could be alerted to serious problems relative to different states within Europe and, if repeated regularly, the survey would enable deterioration or enhancement to be detected over time.

The development of a highly nuanced set of indicators as envisaged here for the UK would not be feasible. Rather the object should be to develop an additional set of core indicators for international application. These would, of course, need to be incorporated as part of the national government set for the purpose of consistency. They would be developed through a process of review of state family wellbeing indicator sets, or approximations thereof, and consideration of the feasibility of standardised data collection. Some level of pan-European public consultation repeated over time might also be possible. The indicators would encompass objective measures relating to, for example, income levels, housing and health across the generations, and subjective measures concerning, for example, perceptions of relationships and emotional wellbeing. This part of the typology would be based on the degree to which states met the indicators specified.

## Benefits of the new typology

One of the principal benefits of this analytical approach is that it offers a conceptual shift, moving away from the use of family policy as a subsidiary tool of other public policy agendas, such as the reduction of poverty, the operation of the welfare state, gender equality or fertility levels. Instead it advances a paradigm that conceives of family policy as an entity in itself with a legitimate and substantive policy aim – to enhance family wellbeing. It moves away from the broad socio-political framework of Esping-Andersen's (1999) classification of entire welfare regimes in accordance with social democratic, liberal and conservative dispositions. It also differs from the overly narrow measures of, for example, levels of social spending and steps taken to facilitate work–life balance. While pertinent, these analyses are constricting, being limited to a single aspect of family policy. They are also largely concerned with family policy's service and fiscal support dimensions, rather than its regulatory functions. In contrast, the typology proposed here is concerned with the aims and realisation of an holistic family wellbeing agenda, engaged with the transparent reconciliation of inter- and intrafamily interests.

The *family wellbeing typology* is a tool that would be concerned not only with classification, but also with publicising a cause and selling an approach. It would be concerned with measuring the degree to which countries move towards a model of family policy that has as its purpose the enhancement of family wellbeing across the generations. The intent to influence policy through comparative analyses is not unusual, and indeed is evident, being only thinly disguised in many typologies. The underlying message in Esping-Andersen's typology of the welfare state is that the social democratic model is optimal; analyses of gender issues clearly have aspirations to enhance women's life choices; and assessment of social spending in family policy have predominantly been undertaken from the perspective that high levels of spending are a good thing. Thus the typology debate is a political one – and that simply requires acknowledgement.

## Overview

In summary, the principal ingredients of the proposed future for progressive family policy are as follows:

- First, family policy needs to be re-oriented away from being the tool of other policy agendas, which have in the past placed an over-ambitious and inappropriate burden of expectation on family services. Instead a family policy should be constructed that has as its core purpose the promotion of family wellbeing across the variety of groups and interests, some aligned and some divergent, that constitute family life. In seeking to promote such wellbeing, there is a need for realism and moderate expectations in managing the tensions that exist in family relations.

- Second, in order to take forward such a family policy, a rights approach is advocated offering transparency in terms of the relationship between the state and families, and the mechanism for weighing up and reconciling different interests within families. Rights establish the basic parameters of state support and regulation, and awareness among individuals and organisations as to what to expect; they can also act as a service driver. They have the potential to set out clearly the regulation of family relationships, to arbitrate fairly and openly, and consequently to reduce tensions. From the negotiation of rights, responsibilities emerge. The process is one of transparency and open negotiation of individual and social interests and associated obligations. Rights and responsibilities are interdependent and, as with rights, family responsibilities should be more clearly defined, including both the caring obligations of adult children for their parents, and those of parents towards their children, possibly through the development of a parenting code. The state's responsibilities similarly require more precise definition.
- The third component relates to the formulation of the objectives of family policy and associated rights, supports and regulation through the development of a set of family wellbeing indicators involving public consultation. This would not be a one-off exercise, but subject to periodic review to take account of changes in expectations of family life. There is an associated proposal to promote awareness and public debate of the moral issues and shifting ethical perspectives that affect family relations, including possibilities for change. This enhanced public understanding and engagement would in turn inform expectations of family life and input into the definition of family wellbeing via the indicator set.

- A final proposal is for the development of a new typology for family policy, which would reflect and provide both an analytical and advocacy tool for this reframed approach to family policy.

# SEVEN

# Conclusion: the proposal and future scenarios

In this concluding chapter the core features of the proposed change in approach to families and public policy are summarised and reviewed in relation to political and economic futures. The nitty-gritty reality of the Coalition government and a possible left-leaning successor government are considered for the purpose of assessing the practicalities of implementation, and the experience of both recent governments – New Labour and the Coalition – are drawn on to inform the exercise.

The all-pervading question for any future programme for families with a service element must be the economic context. Consequently the impact of the proposed re-orientation of family policy is run against different scenarios of economic contraction and growth. Feasibility questions are asked in particular in respect of a period of static or minimal growth, and they include a probing of demand and expectations.

Finally the UK is not an island in terms of political thought or political direction, with supranational bodies in place. The feasibility of these family policy proposals is set in the context of the EU and UN's operations. The differences and alignments of the recommendations in relation to major strands of European family policy are assessed and consideration given as to fit.

## Overview

The decision to write this book was based on the premise that it is worth documenting what has appeared to many to be a remarkable era for family policy, which has now come to an end. The demise of New Labour was perceived in the world of family services as somewhat apocalyptic. While the transition under the Coalition government has not been as momentous as anticipated, it was perhaps the sense that New Labour presented a unique opportunity and period of growth for family services – a flourishing that was distinctive in kind and volume – which made the conclusion of its period in office, to put it frankly, dreaded. The economic downturn sealed a sense of pessimism.

Whatever the final legacy, 1997-2010 was a decade for family policy that was worth the record. Substantial changes were made to the nature of services, and the support and regulation of family life sufficient to constitute a conceptual shift in the role of the state vis-à-vis family relationships deserving of the description 'a revolution'. It is important that the achievements are digested and noted, offering a history rather than a blank canvas. Of course young researchers in today's think-tanks may operate with a dismissive attitude to the past; nevertheless some collective memory may be helpful in fostering future developments. That has been the objective here.

It has not been a detailed analysis of individual projects; other publications have made that important contribution. Rather it has been a broad sweep review of what happened – the multiple themes that emerged and their interface with the realities of the day. It is a record to be proud of, and for those involved in the development of the blueprint during the incubation period of New Labour's time in opposition, a welcome return on and validation of endeavour.

It is in the days of opposition that ideas for the future are conceived and honed by governments in waiting. It is a safe place to cast about and think, without the immediate obligation of having to address the limiting realities of implementation, a time to test the wings of ideas. And it is to this 'testing' enterprise that this book is designed to make a contribution. In addition to providing a thematic history, it is intended to offer a conceptual stimulus for the next phase of progressive family policy. To this end, the analysis has looked at what was wrong as well as what was right.

The problem for New Labour was not in endeavouring too little, but too much, and too much was being asked of family policy. Overly ambitious and simplistic targets were established that could not be met across poverty reduction and social mobility enhancement; there was inadequate consideration of feasibility. While human behaviour can be modified, New Labour failed to recognise significant limitations in terms of the scope of expected change and the length of time needed to change relationships and behaviours across areas such as children's upbringing, anti-social behaviour, and gender and power relations. Most significantly, New Labour tried to use family policy inappropriately as a primary route for tackling economic and social inequality. The macro-economic scale of the problem demanded responses of a similar nature. While tax and benefits were used for income redistribution, there was too great a reliance placed on changes to children's upbringing to achieve social mobility. Measures were needed that would address the structural causes of inequality, such as the traditional high levels of low income employment in the UK, juxtaposed with obscenely high financial rewards at the top of the scale. Furthermore, changing the behaviour of groups of the population was bound to be slow, and the knock-on effect of increasing mobility even slower. There is too great an imperative to redress poverty to allow it to be subject to such a gradualist, limited impact approach.

The Coalition government's policies on families have also been reviewed in the book. They emerge as a paler image of New Labour's family and the state enterprise. There has been contraction that has been substantially in evidence in relation to financial benefits with the associated dangers of increasing the risk of child poverty. This contrasts with New Labour's measures to support income redistribution through the taxation and benefit system. There has been a Coalition tendency to tackle poverty through early childhood interventions – a scaled-down version of New Labour's aspiration for family services. The scaling-down has been achieved through a combination of reduced funding and reduced regulation of expenditure with, for example, the childcare obligations of local authorities being subject to review, and the removal of ring-fenced funding for

Sure Start. Certainly a rights model is far from the Coalition's vision for family services.

Highly pertinent to future scenarios has been the failure of both the New Labour and Coalition governments to develop a family policy that embraces the full range of interests across genders and generations in a sufficiently cohesive fashion to merit the application of the term 'family policy'. Redressing the fragmentary nature of policies should be one of the principal issues to be addressed in the next phase of development.

The proposals put forward in the discussion in this book for a future model draw on what was both positive and realistic in the revolution in family policy under New Labour, as well as its failings. They are established in conceptual and analytical detail with a full rationale in Chapters Five, 'What was wrong?', and Six, 'Looking to the future'. On the positive preservation side they involve maintenance of a significant role for the state in supporting and regulating family relationships, with a continued promotion of a socially liberal perspective and financial and service supports for families. In terms of redressing failings, in addition to requiring that family policy should no longer be viewed as a tool of other government agendas, the model specifies the integrated promotion of family wellbeing from cradle to grave across the full range of groups and interests, some aligned and some divergent, that constitute family life. In delivering this policy, a rights approach is proposed, with clearly defined caring responsibilities, offering transparency in the relationship between the state and the family, and a tried, tested and relatively fair mechanism for weighing up and reconciling different interests within and between families. There are also recommendations that family policy objectives be determined through a process of public consultation establishing a set of family wellbeing indicators, and that public debate and challenge on the moral issues that affect family life be stimulated. Overall the family policy framework envisaged is informed by a scepticism of the enlightenment's conception of the perfectibility of man. Rather than operating with a presumption that 'things are going to get better', the model has been developed in response to the perennial question – 'how are we going to manage the tensions that exist within and between individuals in respect of family relations?'.

The model is projected for the UK, but with some aspiration for wider European influence. The compliance of other European states is far from being a necessity, but the interconnectedness of European life and, in particular, the developing role of international government, renders a broad, cross-border approach a logical option. This is particularly the case bearing in mind the considerable role of human rights in the model and its requirement that family policy be taken away from extraneous and inappropriate government agendas. *Family wellbeing* provides the opportunity for a common principle to be adopted by European states that would enable family policy to come of age with its own rationale, offering a common point of reference for that rather fraught, complex and variable relationship that exists between families and the national and international 'state'.

## Steps

Consequent to this proposed conceptual change the following nine steps are put forward for a revised family policy.

### *Step 1: A statement of family policy*

Clarity and transparency should be at a premium in an area of policy where there are inevitably multiple tensions and interlocking rights and responsibilities with highly interconnected roles for the state, the family and the individual. A statement should be articulated which establishes the need for a family policy, describing its role, scope and underpinning philosophy. Clear enunciation is necessary for open government and to enhance public awareness and debate; it is also needed as a demonstration of government commitment and to set a point of reference for policy making. The statement would provide a marker of a change of approach and intent. It would counter the lack of definition from which family policy currently suffers, and provide the momentum and direction for a new progressive phase.

The philosophical component should acknowledge an underpinning value system concerned with the preservation of human rights, protecting individuals and promoting social justice for families. It should elucidate the significance of families and provide a specification of 'family' in terms of its function within the context of the state and public policy – essentially a caring function, as defined in Chapter One (see p 4). The philosophy should establish the concept of family policy as a tool for promoting family wellbeing through managing 'the family' as the core caring unit of society. This would include the management of mutual and divergent interests within families, and the management of collective interests associated with, for example, generations and genders.

There should be an acknowledgement that, in this management role, policies should be framed with realistic expectations of effecting behavioural change including recognition of the complexities involved and the necessity for compromise. There should also be an appreciation of the need to accommodate shifts in social mores and morality, combining the preservation of a level of stability with a responsive approach.

There should be a clear specification of the parameters of the newly defined family policy, with its focus on delivering the aims described here. In particular, there should be acknowledgement of the move away from using it to support other socio-economic goals.

### Step 2: Family wellbeing indicators

With family wellbeing at the centre of a reframed policy, appropriate family-sensitive delivery tools need to be set in train. As a preliminary step, a set of family wellbeing indicators should be developed through a process of national consultation. As the means for enhancing understanding and measuring family wellbeing over time and responding flexibly to changes in public perception, the indicator set would support planning, implementation and monitoring processes. Underpinned by human rights values, the indicators would span physical, social, economic and psychological domains. There would be objective measures, such as levels of income, and subjective ones, such as feelings about relationships. This concern with family wellbeing would be reflected in a focus on family functioning, mental health issues, the quality of relationships and caring and morality as cast within families. There would be a move away from reliance on the household as an economic unit for measurement, to the caring relationship network. The consultation process envisaged is described in detail in Chapter Six.

### Step 3: Debating shifting morality

The fluidity of morality, changing attitudes and the multiplicity of human motives and impulses that affect relationships and behaviours should be further accommodated by the establishment of an independent think-tank. Its purpose would be to facilitate the investigation, reflection and debate of issues of moment in the sphere of ethics, morality and relationships. Engaging with 'difference', the body should be distanced from government. It should be designed to stimulate change, diminishing the potential for established morality and culture to ossify and act as a force for repression, out of kilter with developing thinking and popular sentiment. Located outside academia, but drawing on academic analysis combined with topicality and policy orientation, this might be a single organisation or a network distributed across existing institutions.

### Step 4: Establish rights and responsibilities

A major exercise in establishing, clarifying and publicising rights and responsibilities relating to families should be undertaken, drawing on an overarching human rights direction for family policy as amplified by the indicators. In order to be functional, the model developed should be confined to core expectations capable of population-wide delivery.

Chapter Six described the benefits to be derived from a rights-based approach, specifically in managing tensions between individuals, across generations and interests, and between families and the state. Financial support, care, the regulation of family relations and property, child protection, criminal justice – all of these are involved. The case has been made that rights spanning these dimensions could act as a relatively transparent and fair arbiter. The exercise proposed here builds on that premise. Corresponding responsibilities of state and individuals would similarly benefit from clarification.

Establishing rights and responsibilities would involve a considerable undertaking across financial and welfare services, family law and criminal justice. It would be particularly taxing in those areas suffering from significant lack of definition, such as the role of parents in bringing up their children, and the role of adult children in supporting their parents – and the relationship of both to the caring and regulatory function of the state. Nevertheless it has been argued in this discussion that the benefits to be derived from greater clarification and cohesion are substantial and outweigh the onerous task of getting to grips with the complexities. Ultimately day-to-day administration would be simplified by this measure, with clearer courses of action and demarcation being readily to hand, in addition to the good of open government.

### Step 5: Reviewing the distribution of resources

In tandem with the establishment of rights, an ongoing review of the distribution of resources across the generations should be instituted. Open consideration of the fairness and direction of national resource allocation has the potential to stimulate the development of a coherent rationale to underpin policies. It would have a positive impact on government culture, bringing some order and transparency to the current somewhat anarchic process of government departments bidding for dwindling resources. As well as rights, the family wellbeing indicators and other components of the family policy process would feed into this deliberation.

### Step 6: Family wellbeing impact statements

In order to enhance awareness and focus government department attention on family policy, there should be a trial of family wellbeing impact statements in respect of current and prospective legislation. The family wellbeing indicator set would provide a point of reference for this tool, and there would also be a link with the rights and responsibilities framework and the resource distribution review.

### Step 7: Service functioning

As well as resource allocation, service functioning requires a whole family orientation. An ongoing exercise should be instituted drawing together examples of best practice in whole family approaches and offering guidance for service development. It would span the multiplicity of public services on the ground including, inter alia, health, social care, education, housing, transport, criminal justice and family law.

### Step 8: A central government coordination role

In order to achieve the living family policy envisaged here, a central government function would be required capable of driving implementation. Its role would encompass matters such as the linking of family wellbeing indicators to impact statements and the development of rights and responsibilities, and there would be a need to engage with human rights and debates on morality. The process of honing family policy would be ongoing, subject to regular reviews and, where appropriate, revision. It would fall to such a central government function to motor and coordinate this process.

### *Step 9: A new analytical tool*

A final measure to reinforce a family policy anchored to the family wellbeing agenda would be the development of an appropriate comparative analytical tool. A new typology is proposed which would reflect the new family policy framework. Operating at an international comparative level it would facilitate the development of family policy not only within this country, but also abroad, particularly in Europe, where pan-European administrative comparisons are highly pertinent.

The typology would assess the degree to which countries have a comprehensive national family policy with the exclusive object of enhancing family wellbeing and reconciling familial tensions. It would include consideration of whether the public is engaged in determining the parameters and expected standards of that wellbeing, and whether policies operate within a transparent framework of rights and responsibilities. It would also measure the degree to which standards of family wellbeing are met.

### Economic inequality

Structural measures to tackle inequality across socio-economic groups – classes – are not a function of the family policy proposed here. However, differentials do have implications for families and their impact should be taken into account in addressing socio-economic relations. The family impact statements and other 'steps' proposed should inform the direction of government travel in the socio-economic sphere, and this might be facilitated by formal liaison arrangements with a government administrative function specifically concerned with reviewing and making recommendations on matters of inequality redress across socio-economic groups.

## Political dimension

There is no insurmountable reason why the proposals outlined here for a refinement of family policy should not be undertaken by either the Coalition government or a future left of centre government. The interest in happiness or wellbeing indicators demonstrated by the current government has the potential to be aligned with the proposed development of family wellbeing indicators. Nevertheless, there are some matters of principle that may present points of difficulty for an administration with a right of centre political persuasion. Redistribution through macro-economic measures, as recommended in Chapter Six, may pall. Certainly there is no evidence to date that such measures would be palatable. As we have seen in Chapter Four reviewing the Coalition's record, the tendency has been to reduce benefits to the less well off; consequently predictions of an increase in child poverty abound (Brewer and Joyce, 2010), and no measures comparable to the introduction of the minimum wage are on the horizon. While New Labour's anti-child poverty legislation has not been removed from the statute book, there are no proposals for measures that will realise its objectives. Rather the Coalition has supported an approach that minimises the significance of income in its discourse on poverty. The early years interventions, on which it is placing considerable reliance, are a watered-down, restricted version of New Labour's endeavours, with Sure Start, childcare and a host of other initiatives curtailed. Private funding for family services and reductions in welfare benefits in order to pay for services, as have been proposed under the Coalition's auspices, would not be within the spirit of the proposals here for a family policy grounded in significant financial redistribution and the institution of entitlements to core family services. A rights-based policy would be unlikely to prove attractive to a right of centre government that has demonstrated its desire to relax obligations to deliver services such as childcare and children's centres. Localism as currently being defined by the Coalition is also a demonstration of an in principle antipathy to citizens' – or families' – rights.

In terms of the progressive left, the failings of the previous government's policy on the family have informed the development of the paradigm floated in this discussion, in particular New Labour's over-ambitious expectations of family policy to deliver on its wider social agenda of poverty reduction, social mobility and social cohesion. Nevertheless, there are positives within the record. In addition to the introduction of the Human Rights Act, the New Labour leap forward in terms of the conception and scale of family services, and its socially liberal measures increasing choices and promoting inclusiveness in family life, were remarkable and should constitute some of the mainstays of the next phase of progressive development.

Building on this creditable record, there is a strong possibility that a reframed left of centre government might adopt and run with the family policy framework proposed here as part of a refreshed brand. And there are indications in the early stages of Labour's recharge that the direction embarked on might fit. Of particular relevance is the undertaking to go beyond redistribution via taxation and benefits to consideration of low pay structural issues, to introduce the 'living wage' above the minimum wage and to regulate for responsible business practices which address the needs of employees (Miliband, 2011a, 2011c). The measures may not go far enough for a major impact on inequalities, but they do suggest an appreciation as to where action needs to take place.

Other aspects of the model proposed in this book, its comprehensive, intergenerational scope and its focus on family wellbeing and rights, would mean a re-orientation that has not featured to date in the public commitments of the Labour opposition. However, in principle there is no obvious incompatibility, and social rights and entitlements did inform the closing days of the New Labour administration.

## Economic backdrop

Political futures are dependent on economic futures. In a period of substantial growth, with political will, services can expand, acquire stability and become part of the national landscape of care. In periods of contraction or minimum growth, choices still exist as to how far care provision is eroded.

There can be no doubt that if a period of economic prosperity was to emerge in four to five years' time, these proposals for family policy would be facilitated – certainly in relation to the services to support family wellbeing. Establishing entitlements in these circumstances would be less worrying for government. There would also be greater potential for government action to reduce poverty through both tax and benefits redistribution and through measures affecting employment conditions. Gender equality in work–home relations would similarly be facilitated. High levels of employment tend to be beneficial to female recruitment. Furthermore, the value of female labour and the availability of resources and reduced economic pressure on employers would make the government's task of regulating employment in favour of equality and a family-friendly environment easier.

That said, economic growth could detract from an appreciation of the need to tackle the fundamentals of inequality, the distribution of resources across classes and generations and the identification of core service needs. This was exemplified in some measure during the New Labour epoch. Soaring incomes were witnessed at the top of the scale, but this was unchallenged because overall a period of plenty translated into tax and benefits gains for the poor. Services grew and the population benefited, but there was no analysis of what essential entitlements should be. Nor was there consideration of the relative distribution of resources across services, and indeed across generations, which would have involved openly addressing the reality of interests, their divergence as well as their convergence.

A period of relative economic stagnation, while offering a negative prospect in many ways, could nevertheless concentrate the political mind so as to develop an open and fair system of resource allocation across population and age groups, supporting the essentials of family life, with a set of family wellbeing indicators providing a transparent and consensual benchmark. Similarly, economic pressure could provide the rationale for establishing greater clarity as to the relative responsibilities of the state and the family in relation to care for both children and other family members, in particular older people. Definitions of levels of entitlement to state support would be part of this process.

A different governmental route might be to fudge responsibility and entitlements with the motive of contracting service provision without full specification. The political pressure during an economic downturn, particularly after a period of significant service investment, may make such a prospect tempting. Ultimately, then, it is a question of conviction and the premium placed on having clarity of relationships in society and openness in government.

There are, of course, some dimensions to family policy that are not resource-dependent, except peripherally. These will function largely independently of economic prospects, unless catastrophe is envisaged. They pertain to the regulation of family relationships, such as marriage, civil partnerships, post-separation caring for children, non-discrimination against same-sex couples, children's agency, the age of maturity, the age of sexual consent, the right to know parentage, human fertilisation and more.

## International context

Having run the proposals for a new family policy aspiration past the challenges of political and economic reality, the third dimension for consideration is the international context.

In terms of international regulation there is a particular synergy between the proposals being forward here and the human rights drivers that operate in the Council of Europe. The rulings of the Court of Human Rights are undertaken in the tradition of a transparent and proportionate weighing up of rights. The opportunity for the individual citizen to have recourse to legal challenge provides a component of reassurance in what might be construed as a David and Goliath relationship between the individual and the state. A broader human rights approach is also advanced as a core point of reference in UN fora, and it informs associated international thinking and exposition of public policy.

Turning to the EU, where the UK has obligations of compliance established by treaty, there are points of emphasis that need to be recognised. Family policy is not per se within the Union's remit. As discussed in Chapter Three, while EU stipulations and commentaries often relate to families, they do so largely from the perspective of its founding purpose – economic and social development, and the free movement of labour and associated need for the equitable treatment of workers. There are examples of directives on the subject of family life, as we have seen, and indeed a reference to the need for comprehensive family policies. Nevertheless, the general direction of travel is concerned with economic perspectives, and this needs to be borne in mind in making EU connections on the family policy front. There are differences between this and a comprehensive family wellbeing-centred model.

Differences also need to be recognised in relation to family policies in individual countries within Europe. The variety of typologies used for the analysis of family policy described in Chapter One revealed the divergent trends that exist across the continent. They encompass the degree to which a social welfare approach has been adopted, the role of the family and the state in relation to caring and other functions, gender relational issues and more. There are also divergences that have perhaps not been assessed in sufficient depth, for example, the different prime interests of governments in their policy dealings with families. We have discussed the degree to which some countries are pre-occupied with fertility issues while others are not. In the UK there has been a unique role accorded to family policy in terms of governmental aspiration to reduce poverty and to increase social mobility through family interventions.

While there have, then, been differences in the nature of and motives behind family policy across Europe, they have, on the whole, proved compatible. And there are also growing similarities, for example, in relation to the provision of services for families, enhanced early years interventions and the move towards gender equality and support systems to facilitate female employment (Blum and Rille-Pfeiffer, 2010). The trend has been towards convergence and there have been many facilitators here including communications, economics and international government. The possible emergence of a different model, with its focus on the promotion of family wellbeing and commitment to the family in the round, could undoubtedly be accommodated within this process of assimilation, while also adding a fresh dynamic and prompt to assess and develop European family policy from a new perspective.

## A final note of caution

The conclusion of this discussion is that the proposition for a revision of family policy is feasible across political, economic and international fronts; feasible, but not easy. It would be an ambitious enterprise that would take some recasting of thought, habit and administration. However, the institution of a genuine family policy, as envisioned here, would constitute a significant governmental achievement.

Sceptics might question the timing, with the thrust of current concerns being geared towards the global economic crisis. Some distraction in these circumstances is inevitable, but there should be a continuing high profile for the family agenda. Family policy operates as an essential feature of government. Care and the regulation of family life, child protection, care for older dependents – these are core functions and should get the attention they deserve. In addition, there is a strong argument to be made that during a time of economic adversity resulting in increased pressures on intimate relationships and caring for the vulnerable, there is a greater imperative to address the role government has in managing the tensions and difficulties in family life. Research into the impact of recessions in the past has shown that they result in an increase in family breakdown and child protection concerns (Hunt, 2010). Youth unemployment, reductions in benefits and the squeeze on living standards will all take their toll on caring obligations. Whether austerity lasts for a few years or a decade or more, the impact on family functioning will be long term because of the knock-on effect of fractured relationships. It therefore behoves government to get the fundamentals of family policy right.

As well as strains forcing the issue, times of adversity demand responses to core questions that might otherwise be avoided – questions around values and fairness – and we have seen in recent months such a shift in the territory of national debate. Solutions that might have been unthinkable in a less challenging context may now be countenanced. The prime example of this can be seen in relation to equality and the redistribution of resources. While in the decade under New Labour these terms were largely taboo, they have now come out of the closet for the progressive left of centre axis. Because things have gone wrong, beliefs more generally are now up for debate and received thought trends challenged. There are indications that the conceptual direction of a transparent and reflexive family policy informed by a coherent set of principles concerned with balancing interests would chime with the move centre stage of values in the debate on progressive government.

A possibly greater obstacle emerges in relation to the 'downsizing' of governmental aspiration proposed in this reframed family policy paradigm. The move to what might be legitimately described as a more modest goal of promoting the realistic enhancement of family wellbeing through the better management of family interests and needs contrasts with the rather more radical and eye-catching hopes to increase social mobility or fight crime or enhance family fertility rates. The question arises as to whether governments can be weaned from using family policy as a vehicle for other government agendas and from having exaggerated expectations of change and impact. Can family policy be sold as having its own *raison d'être*? Conceptual movement is called for, and persuasion that there are benefits to be had from a genuinely family-oriented wing of public policy, with the antagonisms, messy relationships, warts and all, acknowledged and accepted. A commitment to this degree of unglamorous maturity in government will undoubtedly require a hard sell. The contention in this book is that the hard sell is worthwhile; that enhanced understanding and clarity of purpose in the relationship between government and family has benefits that justify the rigour and discomfort of change.

# References

Adam, S. and Brewer, M. (2004) *Supporting families: The financial costs and benefits of children since 1975*, Bristol: The Policy Press.

Age UK (2011a) *Care in crisis: Causes and solutions* (www.ageuk. org.uk).

Age UK (2011b) *Not enough time. What women think about increases in the state pension age*, London: Age UK.

Allen, G. (2011) *Early intervention: Next steps. An independent report to Her Majesty's Government*, London: Cabinet Office.

Andrews, A., Ben-Arieh, A., Carlson, M., Damon, D., Dwek, C., Earls, F., Garcia-Coll, C., Gold, R., Halfon, N., Hart, R., Lerner, R., McEwen, B., Meaney, M., Otford, D., Patrick, D., Pack, M., Trickett, B., Weisner, T. and Zuckerman, B. (2002) *Ecology of child well-being: Advancing the science and science-practice link*, Atlanta, GA: Centre for Child Wellbeing.

Appleton, L. and Byrne, P. (2003) 'Mapping relations between family policy actors', *Social Policy & Society*, vol 2, no 3, pp 211-19.

Apps, J., Reynolds, J., Ashby, V. and Husain, F. (2007) *Family support in Sure Start children's centres*, London: Family and Parenting Institute.

Australian Government, Department of the Prime Minister and Cabinet (2009) *Family impact statement guidelines* (www.dpmc. gov.au/guidelines/).

Barlow, A. Burgoyne, C., Clery, E. and Smithson, J. (2008) 'Cohabitation and the law: myths, money and the media', in A. Park, J. Curtice and K. Thomson (eds) *British social attitudes: The 24th report*, London: Sage Publications, pp 29-51.

Barlow, A., Duncan, S., James, G. and Park, A. (2001) 'Just a piece of paper? Marriage and cohabitation', in A. Park, J. Curtice and K. Thomson (eds) *British social attitudes: The 18th report, Public policy, social ties*, London: Sage Publications, pp 29-57.

Barnes, J., McPherson, K. and Senior, R. (2006) 'The impact on parenting and the home environment of early support to mothers with new babies', *Journal of Children's Services*, vol 1, no 4, December, pp 4-20.

Barrett, H. (2003) *Parenting programmes for families at risk*, London: National Family and Parenting Institute.

Barrett, H. (2004) *UK Family trends*, London: National Family and Parenting Institute.

Barrett, H. (2007) *Evaluating evaluations*, London: Family and Parenting Institute.

Barrett, H. (2008) *Hard to reach families*, London: Family and Parenting Institute.

Baumrind, D. (1967) 'Child care practices anteceding three patterns of pre-school behavior', *Genetic Psychology Monographs*, vol 75, pp 43-88.

BBC (2010) *Early intervention grant is cut by 11%* (www.bbc.co.uk/news/education-11990256)

Beck, U. (1992) *Risk society: Towards a new modernity*, London: Sage Publications.

Bennett, F. and Dornan, P. (2006) *Child benefit: Fit for the future – 60 years of support for children*, London: Child Poverty Action Group.

Blair, T. (1999) 'Beveridge revisited: a welfare state for the 21st century', in R. Walker (ed) *Ending child poverty*, Bristol: The Policy Press, pp 7-18.

Blum, S. and Rille-Pfeiffer, C. (2010) *Major trends of state family policies in Europe* (www.familyplatform.eu).

Boele-Wolki, K. (2007) 'The legal recognition of same-sex relationships within the European Union', *Tulane Law Review*, vol 82, pp 1949-81.

Brewer, M. (2003) *The new tax credits*, London: Institute for Fiscal Studies.

Brewer, M. and Joyce, R. (2010) *Child and working age poverty from 2010 to 2013*, IFS Briefing Note 115, London: Institute for Fiscal Studies (www.ifs.org.uk).

Brewer, M., Muriel, A., Phillips, D. and Sibieta, L. (2009) *Poverty and inequality in the UK: 2009*, London: Institute for Fiscal Studies.

Brown, G. (1999) 'A scar on the nation's soul', *Poverty*, vol 104, pp 8-10.

Brown, G. (2002) Speech to the Labour Party Conference, 30 September (www.guardian.co.uk/politics/).

Buchanan, A. (1999) *What works for troubled children?*, London: Barnardo's.

Cabinet Office (2006) *Fairness and freedom: The final report of the Equalities Review*, London: Cabinet Office (http://archive.cabinetoffice.gov.uk/equalities).

Cabinet Office (2011) *Opening doors, breaking barriers: A strategy for social mobility*, London: Cabinet Office (www.cabinetoffice.gov.uk).

Cameron, D. (2010) Cameron's speech outside No 10 Downing Street as Prime Minister, 11 May (www.guardian.co.uk/politics/).

Cameron, D. (2011) Speech outlining David Cameron's response to the August 2011 riots, 15 August (www.politics.co.uk/).

Castell, S. and Thompson, J. (2007) *Understanding attitudes to poverty in the UK: Getting the public's attention*, York: Joseph Rowntree Foundation.

Chaplin, R., Flatley, J. and Smith, K. (2011) *Crime in England and Wales, 2010/11. Findings from the British Crime Survey and police recorded crime* (www.homeoffice.gov.uk/science-research).

4Children and Daycare Trust (2011) '250 Sure Start children's centres face closure within a year' (www.daycaretrust.org.uk/pages/250-sure-start-childrens-centres-face-closure-within-a-year.html).

*Christian Today* (2007) 'Cardinal tells Blair of opposition to gay adoption', 23 January (www.christiantoday.com/article/cardinal.tells.blair.of.opposition.to.gay.adoption/9242.htm).

Cizek, B. and Richter, R. (2004) *Families in EU-15: Policies, challenges and opportunities*, Vienna: Austrian Institute for Family Studies.

Clark, K. (1969) *Civilisation*, London: John Murray.

Clegg, N. (2011) Parenting speech, 17 January (www.dpm. cabinetoffice.gov.uk/news/).

Coleman, J. (1997) 'The parenting of adolescents in Britain today', *Children & Society*, vol 11, pp 44-52.

Commission on Families and the Wellbeing of Children (2005) *Families and the state: Two-way support and responsibility*, Bristol: The Policy Press.

Commission on Funding of Care and Support (2011) *Fairer care funding. The report of the Commission on Funding of Care and Support* (www.wp.dh.gov.uk/carecommission/).

Committee of Experts on Social Policy for Families and Children (Council of Europe) (2009) *Family policy in Council of Europe member states*, Strasbourg: Council of Europe (www.coe.int).

Commission on Social Justice (1994) *Social justice: Strategies for national renewal*, London: Institute for Public Policy Research.

Conservative Party (2010) *Invitation to join the government of Britain*, Conservative Party manifesto (http://www.conservatives. com/News/News_stories/2010/04/Conservatives_launch_ election_manifesto).

Cooper, A., Hetherington, R. and Katz, I. (2003) *The risk factor. Making the child protection system work for children*, London: Demos.

Cragg, A., Dickens, S., Taylor, C., Henricson, C. and Keep, G. (2002) *Reaching parents: Producing and delivering parent information resources*, London: National Family and Parenting Institute.

Daly, M. (2011) 'What adult male worker model? A critical look at recent social policy reforms in Europe from a gender and family perspective', *Social Politics*, vol 18, no 1, pp 1-23. (http:// sp.oxfordjournals.org/content/)

Darwin, C. (1871) *The descent of man, and selection in relation to sex*, London: John Murray.

Daycare Trust (2010) *The impact of the spending review on childcare*, Policy Briefing, October (www.daycaretrust.org.uk/).

DCSF (Department for Children, Schools and Families) (2007) *The children's plan: Building brighter futures*, London: DCSF.

DCSF (2009a) *Sure Start children's centres – survey of parents* ( www. education.gov.uk/publications/).

DCSF (2009b) 'Government celebrates the opening of 3,000 Sure Start children's centres', Press release, 8 May (www.dcsf. gov.uk/).

DCSF (2010) *Support for all: The families and relationships Green Paper*, London: The Stationery Office.

Deech, Baroness (2010) 'Sisters, there were never such devoted sisters', Gresham College lecture, 2 February (www.gresham. ac.uk/lectures-and-events).

Dex, S. (2003) *Work and family life in the 21st century*, York: Joseph Rowntree Foundation.

DfE (Department for Education) (2010) *Spending review*.

DfE (2011a) *Families in the foundation years* (www.education.gov. uk/publications).

DfE (2011b) 'Nine local areas to trial payment by results in children's centres', Press notice (www.education.gov.uk/news).

DfEE (Department for Education and Employment) (1998) *Meeting the childcare challenge*, London: DfEE.

DfES (Department for Education and Skills) (2007) *Every parent matters*, London: DfES.

DH (Department of Health) (2000a) *Framework for the assessment of children in need and their families*, London: The Stationery Office.

DH (2000b) *The NHS Plan: The government's response to the Royal Commission on Long-Term Care* (www.dh.gov.uk/).

DH (2010) *A vision for adult social care: Capable communities and active citizens* (www.dh.gov.uk/publications/).

Dolvik, J.-E. (2011) 'Nordic hybrid power – politics with markets', in O. Cramme (ed) *Priorities for a new political economy: Memo to the left*, Oslo: Policy Network, pp 39-45.

Donnelly, J. (2003) *Universal human rights in theory and practice*, Ithaca, NY: Cornell University Press.

Duncan, S. and Phillips, M. (2008) 'New families? Tradition and change in modern relationships', in A. Park, J. Curtice and K. Thomson (eds) *British social attitudes: The 24th report*, London: Sage Publications, pp 1-28.

DWP (Department for Work and Pensions) (2003) *United Kingdom national action plan on social inclusion 2003-05* (www. dwp.gov.uk).

DWP (2011) *Households Below Average Income* ( http://www.dwp. gov.uk/research-and-statistics/).

DWP and DfE (2011) *A new approach to child poverty:Tackling the causes of disadvantage and transforming families' lives*, London:The Stationery Office.

EHRC (Equalities and Human Rights Commission) (2011) 'Inquiry reveals failure to protect the rights of older people receiving care at home', Press release (www. equalityhumanrights.com/news).

Elliot, L. and Wintour, P. (2011) Untitled article on child poverty in Labour's final year in government, 12 May (www.guardian. co.uk/society/2011/may/12/labour-final-year-child-poverty-lowest-level-1980s).

Emmerson, C. (2010) Opening remarks by Carl Emmerson at IFS briefing on the October 2010 Spending Review, 21 October (www.ifs.org.uk/budgets/sr2010/opening_remarks.pdf).

Esping-Andersen, G. (1990) *The three worlds of welfare capitalism*, Cambridge: Polity Press.

Esping-Andersen, G. (1999) *Social foundations of postindustrial economies*, Oxford: Oxford University Press.

Etzioni, A. (1993) *The parenting deficit*, London: Demos.

European Commission (2010) *Crime statistics* (www.epp.eurostat. ec.europa.eu).

Eurostat (2009) 'Live births outside marriage: % of live births' (www.ssb.no/eutgm/tps00018).

Family and Parenting Institute (2006) 'Commission in haste, repent at leisure? Evaluations of family preventative services and the implications for the development of policy', Unpublished seminar discussion.

Family and Parenting Institute (2010) *Changes to tax and benefits on families* (www.familyandparenting.org).

Field, F. (2010) *The foundation years: Preventing poor children becoming poor adults. The report of the Independent Review on Poverty and Life Chances*, London: Cabinet Office.

Flatley, J., Kershaw, C. Smith, K., Chaplin, R. and Moon, D. (eds) (2010) *Crime in England and Wales 2009/10*, Home Office Statistical Bulletin 12/10, London: Home Office (www. homeoffice.gov.uk/publications/science-research-statistics/).

Gauthier, A. (1996) *The state and the family. A comparative analysis of family policies in industrialised countries*, Oxford: Clarendon Press.

Gauthier, A. (2002) 'Family policies in industrialised countries: is there convergence?', *Population*, vol 57, no 2, pp 447-74.

Ghate, D. and Hazel, N. (2001) *Parenting in poor environments: Stress, support and coping*, London: Policy Research Bureau.

Ghate, D. and Ramella, M. (2002) *Positive parenting: The national evaluation of the Youth Justice Board's parenting programme*, London: Youth Justice Board for England and Wales.

Glass, N. (2005) 'Surely some mistake?', *The Guardian*, 15 January (www.guardian.co.uk/).

Goodman, A., Myck, M. and Shephard, A. (2003) *Sharing in the nation's prosperity? Pensioner poverty in Britain*, Commentary 93, London: Institute for Fiscal Studies.

Hantrais, L. (2004) *Family policy matters. Responding to family change in Europe*, Bristol: The Policy Press.

Hart, G. (1999) *The funding of marriage support – Main report*, Report to the Lord Chancellor's Department, London: Lord Chancellor's Department.

Haskey, J. (2001) 'Cohabitation in Great Britain: past, present and future trends and attitudes', *Population Trends*, vol 103, pp 4-25.

Henricson, C. (2001) 'Parenting and youth crime', in J. Coleman and D. Roker (eds) *Support for the parents of teenagers*, London: Jessica Kingsley Publishers, pp 57-76.

Henricson, C. (2002) *The future for family services in England and Wales: Consultation responses to the mapping report*, London: National Family and Parenting Institute.

Henricson, C. (2003) *Government and parenting*, London: National Family and Parenting Institute.

Henricson, C. (2007) *The contractual culture and family services: A discussion*, London: Family and Parenting Institute.

Henricson, C. (2008) 'UK family policy: an outline', Presentation to the Council of Europe Technical Seminar on Family Policy, 11-12 September, Paris.

Henricson, C. (2010) 'UK family policy', Presentation at Towards a Parenting Policy Framework for Australia. International Conference, 8 April, Social Policy Research Centre University of New South Wales, Sydney, Australia. (www.sprc.unsw.edu.au)

Henricson, C. and Bainham, A. (2005) *The child and family policy divide*, York: Joseph Rowntree Foundation.

Henricson, C. and Grey, A. (2001) *Understanding discipline: An overview of child discipline practices and their implications for family support*, London: National Family and Parenting Institute.

Henricson, C. and Roker, D. (2000) 'Support for the parents of adolescents: a review', *Journal of Adolescence*, vol 23, pp 763-83.

Henricson, C., Katz, I., Mesie, J., Sandison, M. and Tunstill, J. (2001) *National mapping of family services in England and Wales: A consultation document*, London: National Family and Parenting Institute.

Hicks, J. and Allen, G. (1999) *A century of change: Trends in UK statistics since 1900*, Research Paper 99/111, London: House of Commons.

Hills, J., Sefton, T. and Stewart, K. (2009) *Poverty, inequality and policy since 1997*, York: Joseph Rowntree Foundation.

Hinds, K. and Jarvis, L. (eds) (2000) *The gender gap. British social attitudes: Focusing on diversity – The 17th report*, London: Sage Publications.

Hirsch, D. (2006) *What will it take to end child poverty?*, Summary (www.jrf.org.uk/publications).

HM Government (2010a) *Building the national care service*, White Paper, London: The Stationery Office.

HM Government (2010b) *The Coalition: Our programme for government* (www.cabinetoffice.gov.uk/).

HM Government (2011) *Open public services*, White Paper, London: The Stationery Office.

HM Treasury (2003) *Every child matters*, London: The Stationery Office.

HM Treasury (2010) *Spending review* (www.hm-treasury.gov.uk).

Home Office (1998) *Supporting families: A consultation document*, London: The Stationery Office.

Home Office (2006) *Respect action plan*, London: Home Office.

Home Office (2011) *More effective responses to anti-social behaviour* (www.homeoffice.gov.uk).

Hunt, S. (ed) (2009) *Family trends: British families since the 1950s*, London: Family and Parenting Institute.

Hutton, W. (2011) *Hutton review of fair pay* (www.hm-treasury.gov.uk/).

Ipsos MORI (2006) *Happy families?* (www.ipsos-mori.com/researchpublications/researcharchive/348/Happy-Families.aspx?view=prin/).

James, C. (2009) *Ten years of family policy: 1999-2009*, London: Family and Parenting Institute.

Junger-Tas, J. (1994) 'The changing family and its link with delinquent behaviour', in C. Henricson (ed) *Crime and the family. Conference report*, London: Family Policy Studies Centre, pp 18-25.

Kamerman, S. and Kahn, A. (1978) *Family policy. Government and families in fourteen countries*, New York: Columbia University Press.

Katz, I. and Levine, R. (2010) 'A policy framework for parenting', Presentation at the Towards a Parenting Policy Framework for Australia. International Conference, 8 April, Social Policy Research Centre, University of New South Wales, Sydney, Australia (www.sprc.unsw.edu.au).

Kaufmann, F. (2000) 'Politics and policies towards the family in Europe: a framework and an inquiry into their differences and convergences', in F. Kaufmann, A. Kuijsten, H. Schulze, K. Strohmeier and P. Klaus (eds) *Family life and family policies in Europe. Vol 2, Problems and issues in comparative perspective*, Oxford: Clarendon Press.

Labour Party (1997) *New Labour because Britain deserves better*, Labour Party manifesto (www.labour-party.org.uk/manifestos/).

Laming, Lord (2003) *The Victoria Climbié report*, London: The Stationery Office.

Laming, Lord (2009) *The protection of children in England: A progress report*, London: The Stationery Office.

Lansley, S. (2009) *Life in the middle. The untold story of Britain's average earners*, London: Trades Union Congress.

Law Commission (2011) *Adult social care*, London: The Stationery Office.

Levitas, R. (1998) *The inclusive society? Social exclusion and New Labour*, Basingstoke: Macmillan.

Lewis, J. (1992) 'Gender and the development of welfare regimes', *Journal of European Social Policy*, vol 2, no 3, pp 159-73.

Lewis, J. and Giullari, S. (2005) 'The adult worker model family, gender equality and care: the search for new policy principles and the possibilities and problems of a capabilities approach', *Economy and Society*, vol 34, no 1, pp 76-104.

Lewis, J. and Ostner, I. (1994) *Gender and the evolution of European social policies*, ZeS-Arbeitspapier Nr 4, Bremen: Zentrum für Sozialpolitik.

McAra, L. and McVie, S. (2007) 'Youth justice? The impact of system contact on patterns of desistence from offending', *European Journal of Criminology*, vol 4, no 3, pp 315-45.

McAuley, C., Knapp, M., Beecham, J., McCurry, N. and Steed, M. (2004) *Young families under stress: Outcomes and costs of Home-Start support*, York: Joseph Rowntree Foundation.

McGlynn, C. (2001) 'Families and the European Union Charter of Fundamental Rights: progressive change or entrenching the status quo?', *European Law Review*, vol 26, pp 582-98.

Mandelson, Lord (2009) *Mandelson: Tax not a 'litmus test' of fairness*, Report on Lord Mandelson's address to a Fabian Society seminar on fairness in recession, 19 January (www.nextleft. org/2009/01/mandelson-tax-not-litmus-test-of.html).

May, T. (2011) 'The urgent need for police reform', 16 August (www.homeoffice.gov.uk/).

Melhuish, E., Siraj-Blatchford, I. ,Taggart, B., and Tymms, P. (2007) 'Impact of research on policy', Symposium, British Educational Research Association Annual Conference, 7 September (www.eppe.ioe.ac.uk) (http://eppe.ioe.ac.uk/eppe3-11/eppe3-11papers.htm).

Midgley, M. (1984) *Wickedness*, London: Routledge & Kegan Paul.

Miliband, D. (2006) *Empowerment and the new deal for devolution*, London: Office of the Deputy Prime Minister.

Miliband, E. (2010) Ed Miliband's speech to the CBI, 25 October (www.labour.org.uk).

Miliband, E. (2011a) 'The cost of living crisis facing Britain', Speech to the Resolution Foundation, 1 March (www.labour.org.uk).

Miliband, E. (2011b) Ed Miliband's speech to the Progress Annual Conference, 23 May (www.labour.org.uk).

Miliband, E. (2011c) Labour conference speech, 27 September (www.labour.org.uk).

Moss, P. (2008) 'Making parental leave parental: an overview of policies to increase fathers' use of leave', in P. Moss and M. Korintus (eds) *International review of leave policies and related research 2008*, London: Department for Business, Enterprise and Regulatory Reform, pp 86-91.

Munby, Mr Justice (2006) 'Human rights and social welfare law: the impact of Article 8', Paper presented at the 'Human rights? Transforming services' Conference, London, 27 March.

Munro, E. (2011) *The Munro review of child protection: Final report* (www.education.gov.uk/).

Nacro (National Association for the Care and Resettlement of Offenders) (2004) *Parenting provision in a youth justice context*, London: Nacro.

National Children's Office of Ireland (2005) *State of the nation's children*, Dublin: National Children's Office of Ireland.

National Family and Parenting Institute (1999) *The millennial family*, London: National Family and Parenting Institute.

O'Brien, M. (2004) *Fathers and family support: Promoting involvement and evaluating Impact*, London: National Family and Parenting Institute.

OECD (Organisation for Economic Co-operation and Development) (2005) *Babies and bosses. Reconciling work and family life, vol 4, Canada, Finland, Sweden and the United Kingdom*, Paris: OECD (www.oecd.org).

OECD (2007) *Babies and bosses: Reconciling work and family life. A synthesis of findings for OECD countries*, Paris: OECD Publishing.

OECD (2008a) *Growing unequal? Income distribution and poverty in OECD countries*, Paris: OECD Publishing.

OECD (2008b) *Doing better for families: United Kingdom* (www.oecd.org).

OECD (2008c) *Babies and bosses: Balancing work and family life* (www.oecd.org).

OECD (2011) *Doing better for families* (www.oecd.org).

Ofsted (Office for Standards in Education, Children's Services and Skills) (2009) *The impact of integrated services on children and their families in Sure Start children's centres*, London: Ofsted.

Olsen, R. and Tyers, H. (2004) *Think parent: Supporting disabled parents as parents*, London: National Family and Parenting Institute.

ONS (Office for National Statistics) (2008) *Living arrangements: Marriage is most common form of partnership* (www.statistics.gov.uk).

ONS (2011a) *Measuring national well-being* (www.ons.gov.uk/).

ONS (2011b) *Civil partnership formation numbers increase* (www.statistics.gov.uk).

Osborne, G. (2011) Autumn statement to Parliament (www.hm-treasury.gov.uk).

Ostner, I. (2003) '"Individualisation" – the origins of the concept and its impact on German social policy', *Social Policy & Society*, vol 3, no 1, pp 47-56.

Ostner, I. (2009) 'Farewell to the family as we know it – family policy change in Germany', in W. Lamping and F. Rub (eds) *From Bismarck to conservative universalism? The politics, problems, and prospects of the German welfare state*, Special issue of *German Policy Studies*, vol 5, no 3.

Ostner, I. (2010) 'The success and surprise story of EU gender policies', Presentation to the FAMILYPLATFORM conference Research on Families and Family Policies in Europe, 25-27 May, Barcelona (www.familyplatform.eu).

Page, J., Whitting, G. and McLean, C. (2008) *A review of how fathers can be better recognised and supported through DCSF policy*, London: Department for Children, Schools and Families.

Park, A., Curtice, J., Thomson, K., Phillips, M., Johnson, M. and Clery, E.
(2008) *British social attitudes: the 24th report*, London: Sage

Parton, N. (2008) 'The Change for Children programme in England: towards the preventative-surveillance state', *Journal of Law and Society*, vol 35, no 1, pp 166-87.

Pascall, G. (2006) *Gender and citizenship under New Labour* (eprints. nottingham.ac.uk/810/1/Gender_and_Citizenship.pdf).

Patterson, G. (1994) 'Some alternatives to seven myths about treating families of antisocial children', in C. Henricson (ed) *Crime and the family. Conference report*, London: Family Policy Studies Centre, pp 26-49.

Pedace, L. (2008) *Child wellbeing in England, Scotland and Wales. Comparisons and variations*, London: Family and Parenting Institute.

Prime Minister (2009) *Building Britain's future*, London: The Stationery Office.

Pugh, G., D'Ath, C. and Smith, C. (1994) *Confident parents, confident children. Policy and practice in parent education and support*, London: National Children's Bureau.

Ramey, S. and Ramey, C. (1992) 'Early education, no intervention with disadvantaged children – to what effect?', *Applied and Preventative Psychology*, vol 1, pp 131-40.

Rupp, M., Beier, L., Dechant, A. and Haag, C. (2011) *Research agenda on families and family wellbeing for Europe. Final report* (www.familyplatform.eu).

Rutter, M. (2006) 'Is Sure Start an effective preventative intervention?', *Child and Adolescent Mental Health*, vol 11, pp 135-41.

Ruxton, S. and Bennett, F. (2002) *Including children? Developing a coherent approach to child poverty and social exclusion across Europe*, Brussels: Euronet.

Ruxton, S. and Karim, R. (2001) *Beyond civil rights: Developing economic, social and cultural rights in the UK*, Working Papers of Oxfam GB and Justice, Oxford: Oxfam.

Schubert, K., Hegelich, S. and Bazant, U. (eds) (2009) *The handbook of European welfare systems*, London: Routledge.

Schweinhart, L. and Weikart, D.P. (1993) *Child-initiated learning in preschool: Prevention that works!*, High/Scope Resource, Ypsilanti, MI: High/Scope Press.

Schweinhart, L. and Weikart, D.P. (1997) 'The High/Scope preschool curriculum comparison through age 23', *Early Childhood Research Quarterly*, vol 12, pp 117-43.

Scourfield, J. and Drakeford, M. (2002) 'New Labour and the "problem of men"', *Critical Social Policy*, vol 22, no 4, pp 619-40.

Sen, A. (1992) *Inequality re-examined*, Oxford: Oxford University Press.

Social Exclusion Task Force (2008) *Think family: Improving the life chances of families at risk*, London: Cabinet Office.

Statham, J. (2000) *Outcomes and effectiveness of family support services. A research review*, London: Institute of Education.

Sutherland, H., Sefton, T. and Piachaud, D. (2003) *Poverty in Britain: The impact of government policy since 1997*, York: Joseph Rowntree Foundation.

Sylva, K., Melhuish, E., Sammons, P., Siraj-Blatchford, I. and Taggart, B. (2004) *Effective pre-school provision*, London: Institute of Education.

Thatcher, M. (1987) Interview for *Women's Own* ('No such thing as society'), 31 October (www.margaretthatcher.org/).

Thompson, M., Vinter, L. and Young, V. (2005) *Dads and their babies: Leave arrangements in the first year*, Manchester: Equal Opportunities Commission.

Tickell, C. (2011) *The early years: Foundations for life, health and learning* (www.education.gov.uk/tickellreview).

Toynbee, P. and Walker, D. (2010) 'The Labour years: could have done better', 25 September (www.guardian.co.uk/politics/).

TUC (Trades Union Congress) (2010) *Women and recession* (www.tuc.org.uk/).

UK WBG (Women's Budget Group) (2011) *The impact on women of the budget 2011* (www.wbg.org.uk).

UNCRC (United Nations Committee on the Rights of the Child) (2002) *Consideration of reports submitted by state parties under Article 44 of the Convention. Concluding observations of the Committee on the Rights of the Child: United Kingdom of Great Britain and Northern Ireland* (www.unhchr.ch/tbs/doc.nsf/ (Symbol)/CRC.C.15.Add.188.En?OpenDocument).

Utting, D., Bright, J. and Henricson, C. (1993) *Crime and the family: Improving child rearing and preventing delinquency*, London: Family Policy Studies Centre.

Wall, K., Leitao, M. and Ramos, V. (2010) *Critical review of research on families and family policies in Europe* (www.familyplatform.eu).

Wilkinson, R. and Pickett, K. (2009) *The spirit level: Why more equal societies almost always do better*, London: Allen Lane.

Williams, F. (2004) *Rethinking families*, London: Gulbenkian.

Williams, L. and Jones, A. (2005) *Changing demographics*, London: The Work Foundation.

Wollny, I., Apps, J. and Henricson, C. (2010) *Can government measure family wellbeing?*, London: Family and Parenting Institute.

# Index

*Note:* The letter 'n' following a page number indicates an endnote.

## A

Abortion Act (1967) 35
Adam, S. 29
Adoption and Children Act (2007) 19
adult couples 4, 22, 24, 34, 73, 106, 112
*Adult social care* (Law Commission) 74
adults
　as carers 118–19
　child-adult divide 98–101
　disabled 115–16
　*see also* fathers; mothers; parents; women
age span 8, 97, 100, 103
Age UK 27, 73
Allen, Graham 66–7
Andrews, A. et al 109
antenatal care 21
Anti-Social Behaviour Act (2003) 25, 32
anti-social behaviour advisers 23
Anti-Social Behaviour Orders (ASBOs) 33, 50, 72, 89
Appleton, L. 9
Apps, J. et al 57, 79, 88, 109
Ashby, V. *see* Apps, J. et al
aspirations 147
　Coalition government 77
　downsizing 149
　gender-related 92, 130
　New Labour 5, 12, 13, 37, 41, 44, 52, 80
　Sure Start 82–3, 84–5, 87
attitudes
　to family policy 55–8, 64
　gender related 92, 122
　surveys of 40–1, 46

## B

babies *see* births
'Baby P' child abuse case 31

Bainham, A.: *The child and family policy divide* 48, 101, 116
Barlow, A. et al 40
Barnes, J. et al 85
Barrett, H. 83, 84, 88, 92
Baumrind, D. 57
Bazant, U. *see* Schubert, K. et al
Beecham, J. *see* McAuley, C. et al
behaviours
　criminal 90, 110
　drivers of 122, 123
　manipulation of 25–6, 86–7, 88, 89, 93, 98, 135
　models of 30, 92, 93
　moral 122–5
　outcomes 94, 96–7, 103
Beier, L. *see* Rupp, M. et al
Ben-Arieh, A. *see* Andrews, A. et al
benefits
　children 21, 65
　cuts to 65, 97, 98–9, 143
　housing 65
　older people 27
　targeting 73
　and taxation 29, 43, 65
　and transparency 65
　unemployment 33
　universal 7
Bennett, F. 101
Big Society 70, 71, 74
births
　extra-marital 40
　registration 19, 20
Blair, Tony 11, 82, 89
Blum, S. 6, 8, 125, 126, 147
Brewer, M. 21, 29
Bright, J. *see* Utting, D. et al
British Crime Survey 90
British Public Attitudes Survey (2006) 46
British Social Attitudes Surveys 40, 41
Brown, Gordon 27, 43, 49

Buchanan, A. 56
*Building Britain's future* (Prime Minister) 10–11, 49
*Building the national care service* White Paper 27
Burgoyne, C. *see* Barlow, A. et al
Byrne, P. *see* Appleton, L.

## C

Cabinet Office: *Fairness and freedom: The final report of the Equalities Review* 11
*Opening doors, breaking barriers: A strategy for social mobility* 68
Cameron, David 42
campaigning 44, 59, 67, 80–1 *see also* lobby groups
care
  antenatal 21
  children *see* childcare
  delivery of 70–1, 101
  expenditure on 27
  impact of economic downturns on 148–9
  older people 21, 27–8, 34–5, 36, 73–4, 99, 113, 116
  work–care divide 36, 37, 64–5, 78, 79, 91–3
Carlson, M. *see* Andrews, A. et al
Castell, S. 82
Centre for Social Justice 61
Chaplin, R. *see* Flatley, J. et al
child abuse 26, 31
child–adult divide 98–101
*The child and family policy divide* (Henricson and Bainham) 48, 101, 116
child benefits 21, 65
Child Poverty Act (2010) 22, 66
child protection 26–7, 31–2, 75
  and bureaucracy 71–2, 113
  interventions 113, 119
Child Tax Credits 21, 65, 66, 68
Child Trust Fund 21–2, 65
childcare
  costs 21, 63–4
  processes 117
  provision 18–19, 30–1, 36, 42, 53
  standards 19
Childcare Act (2006) 18–19
children
  adoption 46
  at risk 31, 90

corporal punishment 45
and crime 32–3, 90, 113
diet 57
discipline 25, 33, 89
  smacking 45, 49
early years interventions 9–10, 66–9, 79, 97 *see also* Sure Start
'feral' 89
financial support 78, 98 *see also* child benefits
inequality 80, 96
poverty 68, 101
  Coalition government and 65
  legislation 22, 66
  reduction 11, 12, 21, 22, 28–30, 51, 78, 80–2, 99, 135
rights 44–5, 114
social exclusion 25, 33, 99
welfare 11, 44, 45, 85 *see also* childcare
wellbeing 14, 24
Children Act (1989) 31
Children Act (2004) 24, 44, 45
Children and Young People's Plans 24
Children and Young Person's Act (1933) 32
Children, Young People and Families Grant 24
children's centres 57
  Sure Start 10, 19, 22, 30, 69, 79
children's commissioners 44–5
Children's Plan 24
*The children's plan: Building brighter futures* (DCSF) 24
Children's Rights Alliance for England 44
children's services 98
civil liberties 50, 57, 72
civil partnerships 8, 10, 40–1, 78
Civil Partnerships Act (2005) 20, 62
civil rights 48–9, 114, 128
Cizek, B. 11
Clark, Kenneth: *Civilisation* 124
Clegg, Nick 68
Clery, E. *see* Barlow, A. et al
*The Coalition: Our programme for government* (HM Government)
Coalition government
  aspirations 77
  child protection 71–2
  control 43
  elderly care 73–4
  events influencing 61–2
  family policies 135–6

family services 99, 100
family wellbeing 109–10, 111
human rights 62
maternity leave 18
philosophy 1–2
poverty 97, 136, 143
rights 143
social liberalism 62–4
social mobility 68
work-life balance 63–4
cohabitation 39, 40
Coleman, J. 44
Commission on Families and the
Wellbeing of Children 28, 29–30,
32–3, 50
Commission on Funding of Care and
Support 74
Commission on Social Justice: *Social
justice: Strategies for national renewal*
41, 44, 53
Committee of Experts on Social
Policy for Families and Children
(Council of Europe) 17–18
Common Assessment Framework 26
communitarianism 55, 61
communities
elder care 74
interventions 113
networks 55
rights 117
support 50 *see also* Home Start; Sure
Start
Community Care and Health
(Scotland) Act (2002) 35
Community Protection Orders 72
Community Triggers 72
conditionality 26, 33–4
*Confident parents, confident children*
(Pugh et al) 30
Conservative governments 36
consultations
Anti-Social Behaviour Orders 72
family wellbeing 66, 109, 110, 121,
128, 129, 130, 136, 138–9
smacking ban 45
social care 27, 99
Sure Start 84
Consumer Price Index 65
contracts
parenting 25
schools 25, 33
Cooper, A. et al 31–2, 71
cost-cutting 69–70
Council of Europe 17–18, 146

Council Tax Benefit 65
crime 89–91
interventions 90, 113
youth 89–90
Crime and Disorder Act (1998) 25, 32
Crime Prevention Injunctions 72
Criminal Behaviour Orders 72
criminal justice 25, 32–3, 72–3, 75,
89–91, 113
Criminal Justice Act (1982) 32
criminal responsibility 32–3

**D**

Daly, M. 36
Damon, D. *see* Andrews, A. et al
Darwin, Charles 106, 122
data collection 129
ContactPoint database 26–7, 71–2
D'Ath, C. *see* Pugh, G. et al
Daycare Trust 63–4, 69
DCSF *see* Department for Children,
Schools and Families
Dechant, A. *see* Rupp, M. et al
Deech, Baroness 118
DfE *see* Department for Education
DfEE *see* Department for Education
and Employment
DfES *see* Department for Education
and Skills
Delphi technique 110
Denmark 7
Department for Children, Schools and
Families (DCSF) 18
*A review of how fathers can be better
recognised through DCSF policy*
(Page et al) 91
*Support for all* 10
*The children's plan* 24
Department for Education (DfE)
*Families in the foundation years* 68
*A new approach to child poverty* 66
Department for Education and
Employment (DfEE) *Meeting the
childcare challenge* 18
Department for Education and Skills
(DfES) *Every parent matters* 24, 70
Department for Work and Pensions
(DWP)
*A new approach to child poverty* 66
*Households Below Average Income* 28
*National action plan on social inclusion
2003-05* 99
*Opportunity for all* 99

Department of Health (DH)
*Framework for the assessment of children in need and their families* 11
*The NHS Plan* 27
*A vision for adult social care* 74
deprivation 11, 82, 118 *see also* disadvantage; poverty
Dex, S. 41
DH *see* Department of Health
disabled adults 115–16
disadvantage
cycle of 10
and female employment 93
interventions 87–8
Jarman Index of Social Disadvantage 82
*see also* deprivation; poverty
discipline 25, 33, 89, 108
discrimination
family forms 19–20, 35, 62–3, 121, 146
reducing 47, 49
divorce 40
Dolvik, J.-E. 95
Donnelly, J. 114
Drakeford, M. 23
Duncan, S. 39, *see also* Barlow, A. et al
Dwek, C. *see* Andrews, A. et al
DWP *see* Department for Work and Pensions

**E**

EC *see* European Commission
EHRC *see* Equalities and Human Rights Commission
Earls, C. *see* Andrews, A. et al
early years interventions 9–10, 66–9, 79, 97
Early Intervention Grant 69
*see also* Sure Start
Eastern Europe 8
economy 126, 134, 145–6, 148
Edinburgh study of youth transitions and crime 90
education
foundation years 67–8
pre-school 52, 67
right to 117
*see also* schools
emotions 3, 4, 58, 106
employment: women 36, 41, 42, 43, 64, 92, 97, 144 *see also* work
Employment Act (2002) 18

*Empowerment and the deal for devolution* (Miliband) 49
English Law Commission 119
Equal Opportunities Commission 35
Equal Pay Act (1970) 35
Equality and Human Rights Commission (EHRC) 47, 49, 116
equality
economic impacts on 149
impact statements 116, 117
and marital status 19
*see also* inequality
Equality Act (2010) 91, 111
Equality (Sexual Orientation) Regulations (2007) 20
Esping-Andersen, G. 5, 6, 7, 126, 130
Etzioni, A. 55
Europe 5–9, 17, 142, 147–8
European Commission (EC)
Parental Leave Directive (96/34/EC) 18, 43
Part-Time Work Directive 43
European Convention on Human Rights 35, 47–8, 54, 72, 115, 116–17
European Court of Human Rights 47–8, 146
European Parliament 54
European Union (EU) 5
crime 90
policy links 125–6, 137, 146–7
social inclusion 99
work-life balance 43
Eurostat 40
*Every child matters* (HM Treasury) 10, 24, 70
*Every parent matters* (DfES) 24, 70

**F**

4Children 69
fairness
Coalition government and 66, 71, 74
impact of economic downturns 51, 149
New Labour and 77, 103–4
resource allocation 140, 145
and responsibilities 119, 136
and rights 114, 116–17, 131
*Fairness and freedom: The final report of the Equalities Review* (Cabinet Office) 11
families

at risk 23, 100
breadwinner model 6, 7, 8
control 20, 25–8, 50, 58
de-familialisation of 7
definition 3–4, 106
expenditure 7
formation 19–20, 46–9
'hard to reach' 88
inequalities 96, 107
intergenerational support 99–100,
    103–4, 111, 112, 117, 118–20, 140
responsibilities 131
rights 115, 131
*Families in the foundation years* (DfE) 68
family centres 30
Family and Parenting Institute 66
family impact statements 141
Family Intervention Projects 23, 25
family law 110, 116, 119
family life 116, 131, 136
    regulation 134, 148
Family Nurse Partnerships 23, 67
family policy
    drivers 6, 11, 59, 131
    economics 142, 144–6, 148–9
    Europe 5–9, 17, 142, 147–8
    evaluations 52
    future model 13–14, 133–49
        analytical tool 142
        central government coordination
            role 141
        family policy statements 137–8
        family wellbeing impact statements
            141
        family wellbeing indicators 138–9
        morality 139
        resource distribution 140–1
        rights and responsibilities 139–40
        service functioning 141
    generational differences 3–4, 12, 13,
        36, 59, 73, 74, 79, 99, 103, 112,
        117, 127–8, 136, 138, 140, 145
    international administration 112–13,
        128–9, 137, 142 *see also* European
        Union
    international context 146–8
    multicultural context 14
    New Labour 11–13
    philosophy of 149
    political dimension 142–4
    principles 13–14
    progressive 130–2, 134–5, 143–4

purpose 2–5, 131
regulation 4, 9, 15, 54, 75, 95, 131,
    134–5
rights 115, 131
statement of 137–8
targets 135
transparency 2, 3, 13, 119, 149
typologies 5, 6–9, 125, 132, 142, 147
United Kingdom 6–7, 9–11, 147
family relations
    intergenerational 122
    support 134, 136
    tensions 112, 128, 148
family relationships: regulation 10–11,
    112, 120, 146
family services 22–4, 125, 141
    targets 23, 30, 56, 69–70, 79, 82–5
family support 55–6, 94, 121, 145–6
    child poverty reduction 28–30
    disabled adults 115
    financial 21–2, 64–5, 112
    inequality 96
    older people 27–8
    programmes 88
    and rights 115
    services 22–4, 69–70, 79, 82–5, 125,
        141
'family tests' 73
*Family Trends* 40
family wellbeing 13, 14, 44, 48, 51,
    75, 77
    analytical tools 126–7
    generational differences 109, 111,
        129, 130
    impact statements 110–11, 141, 142
    indicators 66, 77, 108–9, 110, 117,
        121, 128–9, 131, 136, 138–9, 140,
        143, 145
    regulation 131
    standards 128
    transparency 130, 145
    typology 125–30
FAMILYPLATFORM research
    consortium 6, 8, 43, 125
fathers
    childcare 91, 92
    fertilisation treatment 20
    paternity leave 18, 78
    responsibilities 19, 36
    support for 92–3
    *see also* parents
fertility rates 11, 147
    France 6
    Germany 8

United Kingdom 9, 19, 43
fertility treatment 19, 20, 105, 107
Field, Frank 66–7, 67–8, 81, 97
Flatley, J. et al 90, 91
foundation years 67–8
*Framework for the assessment of children in need and their families* (DH) 11
France 6, 7, 8, 118
*The future of family services* (Henricson) 86

**G**

Garcia-Coll, C. *see* Andrews, A. et al
Gauthier, A. 7
gender equality 6
  effects of economy on 144
  Scandinavia 7, 8
  United Kingdom 9
  and work–care divide 36, 91–3
gender relations 91–2
Germany 7, 8
Ghate, D. 56, 57
Gini coefficient of inequality 80
Giullari, S. 91
Glass, Norman 88
Gold, R. *see* Andrews, A. et al
*Government and parenting* (Henricson) 119
governments: coordination role 141
*see also* Coalition government; Labour; New Labour

**H**

Haag, C. *see* Rupp, M. et al
Halfon, N. *see* Andrews, A. et al
Hantrais, L. 8, 126
Hart, Sir Graham 24
Hart, R. *see* Andrews, A. et al
Haskey, J. 39
Hazel, N. 56
Health in Pregnancy Grant 21, 64, 65
health visitors 24
Hegelich, S. *see* Schubert, K. et al
Henricson, C. 48, 56
  *The child and family policy divide* 48, 101, 116
  *The future of family services* 86
  *Government and parenting* 119, 120
  *National mapping of family services in England and Wales* 31, 55 79
  *see also* Utting, D. et al; Wollny, I. et al
Henricson, C. et al 31, 55 79

Hetherington, R. *see* Cooper, A. et al
Hills, J. et al 29
Hirsch, D. 81
HM Government: *Building the national care service* White Paper 27
  *The Coalition* 63, 68, 69
  *Open public services* White Paper 70, 73
HM Treasury: *Every child matters* 10, 24, 70
Home Office
  *Respect action plan* 25
  *More effective responses to anti-social behaviour* 72
  *Supporting Families* 10, 53, 58
home school agreements 33
Home Start 85
home visits 88
homosexuality 19–20, 40–1 *see also* same-sex couples
*Households Below Average Income* (DWP) 28
housing benefits 65
Human Fertilisation and Embryology Act (2008) 20
human relationships: regulation of 10–11, 35, 106–7
human rights 10, 19, 37, 46–9, 108–9, 111, 116, 126, 137, 146
  impact statements 117
  and multiculturalism 47
  voluntary sector 46
Human Rights Act (1998) 19, 20, 35, 44, 49, 72, 111
  Coalition government 62
  criticisms 115
  drivers 131
Hunt, S. 40
Husain, F. *see* Apps, J. et al
Hutton, W. 95

**I**

impact statements
  equalities 116, 117
  family wellbeing 110–11, 141, 142
  human rights 117
  income redistribution 29, 51, 66, 95, 97, 135, 143, 144
  *see also* wages
inequalities 51–2, 94–8
  children 80, 96
  economic 94–6, 135, 142, 144

families 96, 107
Labour party and 144
inhuman and degrading treatment
114, 116
Institute for Fiscal Studies 29, 65, 73
international law *see* European Court
of Human Rights; European
Parliament
interventions
child protection 113, 119
crime 90, 113
disadvantaged families 87–8
early years 9–10, 66–9, 79, 97
*see also* Sure Start
Ireland: family wellbeing 109–11

**J**

James, C. 10, 18, 19, 20, 21, 23, 24, 26,
37n, 78, 83, 92, 100
James, G. *see* Barlow, A. et al
Jarman Index of Social Disadvantage
82
job creation 95
Jones, A. 92
Joseph Rowntree Foundation 81
Junger-Tas, J. 90

**K**

Kahn, A. 7
Kamerman, S. 7
Katrim, R. 48
Katz, I. 36
*see also* Cooper, A. et al; Henricson,
C. et al
Kaufmann, F. 6
Kershaw, C. *see* Flatley, J. et al
Knapp, M. *see* McAuley, C. et al

**L**

Labour
and inequalities 144
and social liberalism 35–6, 63, 120–1
*see also* New Labour
Laming, Lord 26, 31
Lansley, S. 95
law *see* European Court of Human
Rights; European Parliament;
Youth Justice Board
Law Commission: *Adult social care* 74
Lawrence, D.H. 124
leave
maternity 18

parental 18, 43, 92
paternity 18, 78
Leitao, M. *see* Wall, K. et al
Lerner, R. *see* Andrews, A. et al
Levine, R. 36
Levitas, R. 51
Lewis, J. 7, 35-6
Liberal Democrats 63
lobby groups 82
*see also* pressure groups
local authorities
duties 116
parenting strategies 23
*see also* public sector
Local Government Act (1988) 41–2
Local Service Partnerships 49
localism 70, 143

**M**

McAuley, C. et al 85
McCurry, N. *see* McAuley, C. et al
McEwan, B. *see* Andrews, A. et al
McGlynn, C. 54
McLean, C. *see* Page, J. et al
McPherson, K. *see* Barnes, J. et al
Mandelson, Peter 51–2
marriage 19, 40 *see also* civil
partnerships
Marriage and Relationship Support
Grant 24
married couple's allowance 19, 34,
35, 63
maternity grants 21
maternity leave 18
maternity pay 18
Meaney, M. *see* Andrews, A. et al
Melhuish, E. et al 52; *see also* Sylva,
K. et al
Mesie, J. *see* Henricson, C. et al
*Meeting the childcare challenge* (DFEE)
18
Miliband, David: *Empowerment and the
deal for devolution* 49
Miliband, Ed 95, 144
Minimum Income Guarantee 27, 34
Moon, D. *see* Flatley, J. et al
morality 109, 120–4, 123, 139
*More effective responses to anti-social
behaviour* (Home Office) 72
MORI surveys 56
mothers
support for 18, 21, 67 *see also*
childcare

and Sure Start 83
*see also* parents
multiculturalism 14, 47
Munby, Mr Justice 115
Munro, Professor Eileen 71

**N**

NHS *see* National Health Service
*National action plan on social inclusion
2003-05* (DWP) 99
National Care Standards Commission
27
National Children's Bureau 10
National Children's Office of Ireland:
*State of the nation's children* 109
National Family and Parenting
Institute 56
National Health Service (NHS) 27
*A new approach to child poverty* (DWP
and DfE) 66
New Deal for Lone Parents 26, 42, 43
New Labour 11–13, 18, 36
aspirations 5, 13, 37, 41, 44, 52
behaviour manipulation 86, 93, 98
child poverty reduction 28–9, 80
childcare strategy 18
children's rights 43, 45
demise 133, 134
family policy 42–6, 54–5, 78,
98–101, 103, 111, 134, 143–4
public attitudes to 55–8
homosexual rights 19–20
human rights 47
inequalities 94, 98
localism 70
older people's initiatives 27–8
philosophy 1, 2, 10–12, 51
poverty reduction 43, 136
social awareness 41–2
social rights 47–9
Sure Start initiative 22, 93
women 41
*The NHS Plan: The government's
response to the Royal Commission on
Long-Term Care* (DH) 27

**O**

O'Brien, M. 91
OECD *see* Organisation for Economic
Co-operation and Development
Office for National Statistics (ONS)
65, 66, 108–9

Ofsted (Office for Standards in
Education, Children's Services and
Skills) 83
older people
care 21, 27–8, 34–5, 36, 73–4, 99,
116
by adult children 118–19
poverty 78
support 103
*see also* pensioners
Olsen, R. 116
*Open public services* White Paper 70, 73
*Opening doors, breaking barriers: A
strategy for social mobility* (Cabinet
Office) 68
*Opportunity for all* (DWP) 99
Organisation for Economic Co-
operation and Development
(OECD) 96
Ostner, I. 7
Otford, D. *see* Andrews, A. et al
outreach work 88

**P**

Pack, M. *see* Andrews, A. et al
Page, J. et al: *A review of how fathers can
be better recognised through DCSF
policy* 91
parent advisers 23
parent-child relationship 10, 122
parental leave 18, 43, 92
Parental Leave Directive (96/34/
EC) 43
parenting 94
authoritative 57
and crime 55
parenting code 120, 131
Parenting Contracts 25
Parenting Forum (later Parenting
UK) 10
Parenting Fund 23
parenting groups 22, 56
Parenting Orders 25, 32, 50, 57, 72,
89, 113
parenting programmes 10, 52, 56–7,
88, 100
evaluations 30, 56–7, 80, 82, 83–4
parenting strategies 23, 91
Parenting UK (formerly Parenting
Forum) 10
parents
lone 26, 34, 42, 68, 78
responsibilities 19, 32, 33, 34, 57–8

single 26, 42
support 22–4, 26, 30–1, 67, 99–100
Sure Start evaluations 85
Park, A. *see* Barlow, A. et al
part-time work 92
Part-Time Work Directive (EC)
  (1997) 43
partners
  same-sex 20
  of single parents 26, 34
  *see also* civil partnerships;
  cohabitation
Parton, N. 9
Pascall, G. 36, 63
paternity leave 18, 78
Patrick, D. *see* Andrews, A. et al
Patterson, Gerald 87–8
pay
  legislation 35
  low 95, 98, 144
  maternity 18
Pedace, L. 11
pensioners 27, 29, 34, 99 *see also* older
  people
pensions, state 73
Pensions Bill (2011) 73
Perry Pre-School Project (United
  States) 9–10, 84, 88
personal development 52, 66, 67
personal relationships 10, 12
  *see also* family relationships
Phillips, M. 39
Piachaud, D. *see* Sutherland, H. et al
Pickett, K. 97
police 72
poverty 90, 135
  children 11, 12, 28–30, 34, 65, 68,
    78, 80–2, 99, 101, 135
  cycle of 12
  and employment 42
  ethical perspective 97
  intergenerational 101
  older people 27, 34, 78
  pensioners 27, 29, 34
  targets 12, 51, 80–2, 135
  *see also* deprivation; disadvantage
pre-school education 52, 67
pre-school projects: United States
  9–10, 84, 88 *see also* Sure Start
pregnancy grants 21, 64, 65
pressure groups 44
  *see also* lobby groups
Prime Minister: *Building Britain's future*
  10-11, 49

progressive politics 1–2, 12, 105
  assessments 80
  European Union 43
  lobby groups 82
  New Labour 86, 149
  and reform 20
progressive thinkers 124
public policy 3, 5, 12, 13, 53, 107,
  108–10, 149
public sector: transparency 95, 100,
  101, 103 *see also* local authorities
Pugh, G. et al: *Confident parents,
  confident children* 30

**R**
Ramella, M. 57
Ramey, S. and Ramey, C. 88
Ramos, V. *see* Wall, K. et al
redistribution policies 52, 99, 101
  attitudes to 64
  family wellbeing 107
  income 29, 51, 66, 95, 97, 135, 143,
    144
  resources 82, 143, 149
relationships
  family 112, 120, 146
  human 10–11, 35, 106–7
  personal 10, 12
resource distribution 103, 140–1, 143,
  145
*Respect action plan* (Home Office) 25
responsibilities
  families 118–19, 131
  fathers 19, 36
  parents 19, 32, 33, 34, 57–8, 119–20
  and rights 115, 117–18, 139–40
*A review of how fathers can be better
  recognised through DCSF policy*
  (Page et al) 91
Reynolds, J. *see* Apps, J. et al
Richter, R. 11
rights 114–17, 131, 143, 146
  children 44–5, 114
  civil 48–9, 114, 128
  and responsibilities 115, 117, 139–40
  social 47–9, 114, 128
  and transparency 114, 115, 116–17,
    120, 121, 131, 136, 137, 140, 142,
    146
  universal 47, 48, 115
  and welfare 114, 115
  *see also* human rights

Rille-Pfeiffer, C. 6, 8, 125, 126, 147
riots (August 2011) 72, 90
Royal Commission on Long-Term
    Care 27
Rupp, M. et al 128-9
Rutter, M. 83, 84
Ruxton, S. 48, 101

**S**

Safeguarding Adults Boards 74
same-sex couples *see also*
    homosexuality
    and adoption 46
    civil partnerships 8, 10, 40-1
    rights of 19-20
Sammons, P. *see* Sylva, K. et al
Sandison, M. *see* Henricson, C. et al
Sartre, Jean-Paul 124
Scandinavia 6, 7, 8
schools
    contracts 25, 33
    exclusions 25
    extended 23
    meals 57
Schubert, K. et al 7
Schweinhart, L. 10
Scotland: older people 35
Scourfield, J. 23
Sefton, T. *see* Hills, J. et al; Sutherland,
    H. et al
Sen, A. 11
Senior, R. *see* Barnes, J. et al
sex, pre-marital 40, 41
sex discrimination 20
Sex Discrimination Act (1975) 35
Sexual Offences Act (1967) 35
sexuality 123 *see also* homosexuality
Singapore 118
Siraj-Blatchford, I. *see* Melhuish, E. et
    al; Sylva, K. et al
smacking 45, 49
Smith, C. *see* Pugh, G.
Smith, K. *see* Flatley, J. et al
Smithson, J. *see* Barlow, A. et al
social care *see* care; childcare
social cohesion 105
    achievement of 52, 53, 117, 144
    and criminal justice system 89
    delivery of 11
    promotion of 51, 59
    and social inequality 97
social exclusion
    children 25, 33, 99

reducing 11, 34
    tensions 51-3, 59
Social Exclusion Task Force: *Think
    family: Improving the life chances of
    families at risk* 23, 100
social fragmentation 55
social inclusion 99
social instincts 122-4
*Social justice: Strategies for national
    renewal* (Commission on Social
    Justice) 41
social liberalism 17-19, 35-6, 37,
    39-50, 78
    children's rights 44-5
    Coalition government 62-4
    family formation 46-9
    Labour governments 35-6, 63,
    120-1
    support and control 49-50
    work-life balance 42-3
social mobility 52, 68, 135
social policies 5-6
    and human rights 49, 116
social rights 47-9, 114, 128
social standards 55
social work: child abuse 31-2
Spain 8
Spending Review (2010) 73
*State of the nation's children* (National
    Children's Office of Ireland) 109
Statham, J. 56
Steed, M. *see* McAuley, C. et al
Stewart, K. *see* Hills, J. et al
Straw, Jack 58
*Supernanny* (TV programme) 56
*Support for All* (DCSF) 10
*Supporting Families* (Home Office) 10,
    53, 58
Sure Start 22, 24, 82-4, 87-8, 88-9
Sure Start children's centres 10, 19, 22,
    30, 69, 79
Sure Start Maternity Grant 21
Sutherland, H. et al 98-9
Sweden 104n1
Sylva, K. et al 52

**T**

Taggart, B. *see* Melhuish, E. et al; Sylva,
    K. et al
targets 31, 48, 49, 102, 135
    behaviour 108
    child-focused 12, 51, 80-2, 100
    failure of 85-6

family services 23, 30, 56, 69–70,
   79, 82–5
   Sure Start 83
   transparency 102
   United States 9–10
tax credits 18, 21
taxation
   and benefits 29, 43
   and marital status 19
   and poverty reduction 97
   Value Added Tax 66
   and wealth 51–2
television programmes 56
tensions 4–5
   and adult services 74
   and family relations 112, 128, 148
   of human motives 123
   management of 13, 14, 107, 111–20,
      121
      responsibilities 117–18
      rights 114–17
   and poverty 100–1
   and smacking 49
   and social exclusion 51–3
   and social liberalism 50
   of state involvement 57
Thatcher, Margaret 55
*Think family: Improving the life chances
   of families at risk* (Social Exclusion
   Task Force) 23, 100
Thompson, J. 82
Thompson, M. et al 92
Tickell, C. 68
Toynbee, Polly 80
Trades Union Congress (TUC) 95
transparency
   benefit decisions 65
   family policy 3, 13, 119, 149
   family wellbeing 130, 145
   public sector 95, 100, 101, 103
   rights 114, 115, 116–17, 120, 121,
      131, 136, 137, 140, 142, 146
   targets 102
Trickett, B. *see* Andrews, A. et al
TUC *see* Trades Union Congress
Tunstill, J. *see* Henricson, C. et al
Tyers, H. 116
Tymms, P. *see* Melhuish, E. et al

**U**

unemployment benefits 33
United Nations (UN): and human
   rights 146

United Nations Committee on the
   Rights of the Child (UNCRC)
   44–5, 112
United Nations Convention on the
   Rights of the Child 112–13, 115
United States: Perry Pre-School
   Project 9–10, 84, 88
universal rights 47, 48, 115
universality
   children's services 21–2
   family services 55
   of morality 122
   personal care 27
   rights 47, 48, 115
   Sure Start 22, 30–1, 69
   welfare state 9
Utting, D. et al 10, 55

**V**

Value Added Tax (VAT) 66
values
   and care ethic 108
   and childhood 101
   and family wellbeing 78, 108–9, 139
   and human rights 46–7, 138
   impact of economic downturns 149
   and resource allocation 100
*A vision for adult care: Capable
   communities and active citizens* (DH)
   73
Vinter, L. *see* Thompson, M. et al
voluntary sector
   Big Society and 70, 71
   and human rights 46
   and parental support 22–3, 26

**W**

wages
   legislation 18, 35
   living 95, 103, 144
   minimum 98
   *see also* income
Walker, David 80
Wall, K. et al 6
Weikart, D. 10
Weisner, T. *see* Andrews, A. et al
welfare 3, 5, 43, 49
   children 11, 44, 45, 85
   and rights 114, 115
Welfare Reform Act (2010) 26
welfare states 127
   Esping-Andersen's classification of
      126, 130

Europe 5–7
United Kingdom 9, 51, 73
wellbeing 11, 66, 67
  children 14, 24
  definition 109–10
  families 6, 13, 14, 44, 48, 51, 75, 77,
    107–11
  impact statements 110–11, 141,
    142
  indicators 66, 77, 108–9, 110, 117,
    121, 128–9, 131, 136, 138–9,
    140, 143, 145
  standards 128
  statement on 138
  typology of 125–30
  national 95
Whitting, G. *see* Page, J.
Wilkinson, R. 97
Williams, F. 114
Williams, L. 92
Wollny, I. et al 109
women
  employment 36, 41, 42, 43, 64, 92,
    97, 144
  pregnancy grants 21, 64, 65
  state pensions 73
  *see also* mothers
work 42–3
  and parental responsibility 112, 113
  patterns of 17–19, 91–2
    part-time 43, 92
  and pensions 73
  single parents and 26
  training for 68
  women and *see* women: employment
  *see also* employment; family
    relationships: breadwinner model
Work and Families Act (2006) 18
work–care divide 36, 37, 64–5, 78, 79,
  91–3
Work-Focused Interviews 26
work–life balance 6, 8, 10, 18, 35–6,
  42–3, 54, 63–4, 78, 130, 145
workforce
  demoralisation 84
  inequalities 96, 147
  mothers 97
Working Tax Credit 21, 42, 63, 68

**Y**

young offenders 89
Young, V. *see* Thompson, M. et al
Youth Justice Board 89

**Z**

Zuckerman, B. *see* Andrews, A. et al